Everyday Moments

Lessons that Transform Lives

Melahni Qualls Ake

Kelly Ekwurzel, Kris May, Jodi Bondy
Angie Wood, Stacia Jones, Stefany Dolan,
Shelly Bays, Joyce Brown and Shauna Snyder

Melahni Qualls Ake, et. al.

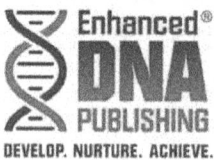

Denola M. Burton
www.EnhancedDNAPublishing.com
info@enhanceddna1.com

Everyday Moments
Lessons that Transform Lives
Copyright © 2024 Melahni Ake

All rights reserved.

No portion of this publication may be reproduced, stored in any electronic system, or transmitted in any form or by any means without the written permission from the author. Brief quotations may be used in literary reviews.

ISBN: 978-1-7378090-8-1
Library of Congress Number: 2024909499

DEDICATION

This book is dedicated to:

My Mentor John Maxwell, who introduced me to the process of personal growth and challenged me to apply these principles to experience growth in my heart that is transforming my life.

My father, John Qualls, who's DNA gave me the gift of curiosity to see the world differently and search for life's meaning.

The Everyday Leaders morning devotional community who together have created a safe place where believers can grow in our faith, every single day.

INTRODUCTION

"Everyday Moments: Lessons that Transform Lives" is a poignant anthology, weaving together the voices of inspiring women spanning six decades. Through heartfelt reflections, these women share profound insights drawn from their life experiences, offering wisdom that touches hearts and uplifts souls. This collection transcends mere storytelling; it navigates the intricacies of life's tapestry, with each contributor imparting invaluable lessons resonant with readers seeking purpose and growth. From triumphing over adversity to savoring moments of joy, the narratives within this book celebrate the diverse richness of human existence.

Delving into insightful chapters, readers embark on a journey of self-discovery and empowerment. "Maximize Your Moments" encourages seizing the present, while "The Way It Was" reflects on the past with gratitude. "It Is the Little Things" underscores the power of small acts of kindness, and "GIFTS" prompts gratitude for life's blessings often overlooked.

"Finding Joy in the Impossible" challenges conventional thinking, illustrating how resilience can lead to unexpected triumphs. Acknowledging life's inevitable challenges, "Life Happens" offers wisdom for navigating its twists and turns, while "A Future and a Hope" instills optimism amidst uncertainty.

"A Doubtful Voice Turned Confident" chronicles the transformative journey from doubt to self-belief, and "From Idea to Impact" showcases how one family's vision transforms lives. "Against All

Odds, But God!" stands as a testament to human resilience and faith in adversity.

Through each chapter, "Everyday Moments" illuminates a path of personal growth and fulfillment, offering hope and inspiration to readers. As readers delve into these pages, they're invited to explore the value of their own life stories and embrace their potential as catalysts for positive change, both in their lives and the lives of others.

Melahni Ake
EVERYDAY LEADERS

TABLE OF CONTENTS

DEDICATION iii
INTRODUCTION v
FOREWORD ix
MAXIMIZE YOUR MOMENTS 3
THE WAY IT WAS 19
IT IS THE LITTLE THINGS 29
GIFTS 41
FINDING *JOY* IN THE IMPOSSIBLE 51
LIFE HAPPENS 63
A FUTURE AND A HOPE 79
A DOUBTFUL VOICE TURNED CONFIDENT 93
FROM IDEA TO IMPACT: HOW ONE FAMILY'S IDEA IS TRANSFORMING LIVES 105
AGAINST ALL ODDS, BUT GOD! 121
EVERYDAY LEADERS 131

FOREWORD

By: Bonnie Schoun

*F*orward, often confused with *Foreword*, is the one word I would select if I used just one word, rather than 365, to write the Foreword to this *Everyday Moments* book. I smile recalling how I first understood that Melahni Ake holds "everyday" in her REAL heart, not just in her red logo for *Everyday Leaders*.

On a Memorial Day weekend, I was surprised to hear, "Good morning, Bonnie!" at 7:30 a.m. [EST]. Melahni's cheerful voice welcomed me to my first Everyday Leaders Devotional Zoom call, hosted 365 days a year.

Hearts aren't just stickers & stationary stuff but genuine life stuff for her. I attest that her example of being an everyday person, committed to encouraging the personal potential in the everyday people around her, consistently influences me to grow forward.

Her everyday moment decision to begin hosting a daily devotional Bible reading, and to move her own faith forward has impacted me every day since I first met her.
Having a place to start every day and a community that cultivates a forward outlook on life has been very enriching and encouraging.

We all need forward encouragement from each other now and then, don't we? Sometimes we feel stuck, lost, like we're going in circles, or just plain too tired to move much at all.

There is help and healing in the hearing of other everyday people's experiences. Encouragement is found from the everyday moments of other women.

Of course, the personalities, experience, and influences will vary throughout this book. The 'volume' and 'accent' may change. Yet the reader can expect to hear a clear and consistent word spoken through this book. "Forward!" is the message voiced by these women, each with her own tone of voice.

Melahni's WHY is challenge. I know her heart motivating the work required to coordinate a meaningful book project such as this. She wants to challenge each reader to consider how the lessons of gifts, hope, love, pain, vision, clarity, and courage each offer inspiration for moving forward in one's own everyday life experience.

Bonnie Schoun

MEET MELAHNI AKE

Melahni Ake is a dynamic and visionary leader passionate about driving positive change in various spheres of life. She graduated from Greenwood High School, where she was a catalyst for collaborating to start the first girls' softball team and radio program. She holds a bachelor's and associate degree from UIndy in Business Administration and Psychology. She is a certified speaker, coach, and trainer with John Maxwell's Maxwell Leadership Team and the first WHY Affiliate Coach in the US. Intentionality has been the driving force for her life's work, spending over twenty-five years in sales, sales training, and executive leadership in the medical device industry. Her strategic approach to life was developed by playing ice hockey in an all-boys league for over twelve years developing her strategic mindset. Her confidence comes from challenging herself and others to make a difference every day. Melahni has founded and led several successful ventures and start-ups, leveraging her entrepreneurial spirit and strategic insight to create innovative solutions for today's challenges.

She is a wife, daughter, athlete, founder, co-founder, board member, author, co-author, podcast host, content creator, social media influencer and advocate, community builder, entrepreneur, and a visionary leader who believes in the power of using our voice to make a greater impact. She's been married to her husband Joe for 33 years.

Melahni is a dedicated advocate for social causes and actively engages in community service and philanthropy. Her unwavering commitment to social impact has earned her recognition as a change-maker and a role model and in 2024 was recognized by Aspire Johnson County as Woman Leader of the Year and her company Everyday Leaders was a finalist for the Champion for Women in 2023 and 2024. Melahni Ake is a true catalyst for change; her journey is a testament to the difference one can make in the world once you take that first action step.

You can connect to Melahni for Keynotes, Speaking, Emcee, Community Event Host, Business Consulting, Personal Growth, Professional Development Workshops, or even be a guest on the Everyday Leaders Podcast.

Find out more at www.everydayleaders.com.

MAXIMIZE YOUR MOMENTS

By: Melahni Ake

In 2016, I was working as a sales and marketing executive with a leading global infection control and medical device company. My everyday experiences included collaborating with physician influencers, key opinion leaders, and sales teams to gain feedback on medical devices used on patients. The physicians were world-class research doctors solving complex disease challenges and improving patient care. My sales teams were both domestic and international. I absolutely loved what I did in the healthcare space. Every conversation was built on gaining feedback and momentum to provide better patient outcomes. I was a bridge to the teams' success and was surrounded by an ever-changing growth mindset environment. It was a time in my life when I was invested in my career because I was contributing to making a difference in people's lives and I felt like every day I had an opportunity to add value. I believe my passion to partner with and help create solutions to treat diseases comes from my experience with personal loss. My dad was diagnosed with late-stage lung cancer when he was just twenty-nine years old. I was just five. As my mom recalls memories, and I read my grandmother's diaries of this time, my heart breaks for what our family experienced. We were not prepared for a terminal diagnosis. My dad had decided to cancel his life insurance just before he was diagnosed. He was in-between jobs, and he couldn't afford the premiums.

Every time we have a painful experience, we begin to understand more about ourselves.

All my life I wondered if the doctors would have been able to find his cancer sooner if he would have had a better outcome. My father only lived a few short months after his diagnosis. Just ten days before Christmas in 1973, he passed away at the age of thirty. Defining moments like this create memories in our hearts that can never be forgotten. Memories are our treasures from joy and pain. Some people get stuck for their entire lives in the memories of their pain, and that can be a very scary and lonely place. Even though I have had painful experiences, I was surrounded by an inner circle of special people that protected my heart and challenged me to grow through the pain.

My grandparents, Paul and Mae Qualls, were my paternal grandparents. They invested in me, mentored me, and loved me. After my father passed away, they stepped into an even bigger role in my life. I have never had my own children, so I can't even pretend to imagine the pain of experiencing the loss of a child. I think it's natural that, as their only connection to my father, they wanted to maximize the potential for my life. They knew that staying close to me, exposing my heart to God was the best way to influence me. As I grew older, their impact on my life grew stronger day by day. As song evangelists, they exposed me to a life of servant leadership, traveling from city to city around the United States, sharing God's Love. As a child, I loved traveling with them and experiencing camp meetings.

My mother was a nurse and worked the day shift from 7:00 a.m. - 3:30 p.m. at St. Francis Hospital. After my father died, my grandparents helped provide a safe place for me during summer vacation, relieving my mom from the expense of childcare. For many years, I spent the summers with them in Orlando, Florida. I looked forward to the last day of school when my grandfather would be in the driveway to pick me up, and we would start our road trip south for the summer. My grandfather was a sought-after song evangelist, and my grandmother would often join him as his accompanist on the piano. His "slate" was full. He made his living serving the Lord through singing at revivals and church camps around the United States. He was booked in many cities for years at a time. It's incredible to believe that he lived his life out of a suitcase. He moved every ten days to a new location singing about Jesus. I have a video recording of my grandfather's testimony. He said, "I never would leave my wife and three boys and sing songs like, "Honey aren't you coming out tonight". I would not trade a celebrity life to do what I do. I love Jesus, and he is the reason I live this life. I want everyone to know about Jesus."

My grandparents loved Jesus. They lived their life to testify and to help save others. If you ever had the opportunity to meet them, you would have loved them, too. No matter where you were you could feel their love in the room. As a child, I loved being in their presence, receiving their love, and learning from those in their inner circle. I was a keen observer. What I knew was my experiences with my grandparents at these camps made my heart happy. It gave me a peace and purpose that I couldn't explain; I just knew it was something that I needed to keep in my life.

Steve Jobs said, "You don't understand your life until you can go back and connect the dots." It wasn't until many years later as I began to understand how important these experiences were. I was living my life differently from my grandparents or my mother. I was working in the medical device industry for over twenty-five years in sales and sales leadership. It wasn't until I was blindsided and eliminated that I began to understand that I was not designed for this kind of pain. This is not the way I wanted to spend the rest of my career — chasing egos in exchange for my life. What I realized is that I spent my entire career building relationships and community, giving every moment of my time and talent to activities that only provided financial stability. This experience taught me the lesson of head vs heart. My heart was broken and empty when I was eliminated. I was traumatized. I had to grow through the next phase of my life to begin to realize how God exposes you to grow every day. This was one of those days to grow. What I learned was I had grown professionally over twenty-five years. I had grown my head by using my heart to serve others. The lesson that changed my life was, as my grandparents who were my mentors had passed away, I had forgotten to invest in personal development to grow myself.

It wasn't until 2016, when I joined the John Maxwell Team that I was spiritually led to invest in growing myself so that I could grow my heart, my purpose, and my significance in the world. As my grandparents always taught me, when we choose to follow God, He will show us how to grow our hearts to serve others.

My memories of traveling to church camps with my grandparents were special. My favorite camps were Beulah Camp in Excel, Alabama, Hartselle, Alabama, and Gaskin Springs, Georgia. Beulah Camp was located on an old country road. I remember driving in our car and pulling a little camper all the way from Orlando to set up for ten days of services. When we would arrive on site, my grandfather would hook up the camper where he and my grandmother would stay, and I would head off to the dormitories across the campgrounds to visit with my friends from previous years. These were special times. We focused on spending time together, to grow together, and these church camps provided a safe place for me to grow. Anyone that has a memory of going to camp every year can appreciate the open tabernacles, sawdust floors, concrete dorms, and echoes of the dinner bell being rung for breakfast, lunch, and supper. My grandparents were incredible mentors that modeled a life of faith ministry and encouraged me to carry this as a vision for my heart. When my grandparents passed, I fell out of the familiar routine of living in my simple faith. They were the ones I watched read their Bible and pray every day. They had extraordinary faith. I was able to borrow theirs while they were alive instead of establishing my own. When the people that shape our beliefs and our lives die, it requires a new level of growth to sustain our confidence and maximize our momentum. Their commitment to their lives was displayed through their consistent choices and purposed mission. Unless you intentionally surround yourself with mentors who keep you accountable and consistently growing, you won't.

In life's simplicity, one borrows beliefs.

In its richness, one owns them.

It was easy for me to grow when someone was leading me, yet I wasn't at a point in my life where I had a capacity to grow myself. When I experienced a sudden job change and elimination, something that was out of my control, I had to develop a new strategy to live my life. I could not grow in this area. I was so traumatized by the corporate manipulation that I experienced a panic attack for the first time in my life. I ended up in the hospital for three days. Uncontrollable stress can cause a panic attack. I had never experienced this kind of stress until this moment. While I was experiencing this new level of emotional trauma, I began doing what I believe a lot of people do in the same situation — reflect.

What I know is that implementing a personal growth and development plan, allowed me to turn my pain into purpose.

I had joined the John Maxwell Team eighteen months prior. I was learning about how to grow personally for the first time in my life. I was inspired to hang my shingle in 2016. After attending the International Maxwell Certification event in 2017, I knew there was something more I needed to grow into. In the fall of 2017, the vision for my *Everyday Leaders 50in50* Podcast became a reality. On my fiftieth birthday, January 12, 2018, with the help of my husband, who is a media producer, we launched our first production together. The purpose of this project was to help me fuel my growth, connect to mentors that would inspire my curiosity, and keep me accountable to consistency. I was studying a book by John Maxwell, *The 15 Invaluable Laws of Growth*. I was laser focused on personal growth. I wanted to learn the strategies other people were applying to overcome obstacles in their lives. I became an avid learner in growth strategies, taking copious notes from every interview, and thirsting for more. This growth process ignited my passion for journalism that I once had in high school. In high school, I was the newspaper editor and helped to start our radio program with Andy Chanley, who is now a popular DJ in Los Angeles. I started attending Ball State University, hoping to become the next Jane Pauley. My life changed, and opportunities drew me away from my gifts until later.

Real growth changes you from the inside.

When I was eliminated, even though I was starting to understand personal growth, I didn't have tools to deconstruct my emotions from reality. I absorbed what was happening to me. It triggered me to question my value.

John Maxwell says, "Reflection turns experience into insight, and evaluated experience is the best teacher."

I remember doing a Facebook live the first week of my reflection. It was during this live monologue, talking through my pain, that my brain began feeling empathy for my mom. It was like a flashback came rushing through my body. I believe it was a moment of clarity and growth. This rush of emotions was stirring inside of me. I didn't know why. My mom and I had always had a good relationship. However on this day, at this moment, something changed. As I was growing up there were things in my heart that I held against my mom; deeply rooted feelings that I had never spoken about. I was holding her responsible for decisions that she made that I didn't agree with. Let me say that again, I was holding her responsible for decisions she made that I didn't agree with. At this moment of my own despair, I was able to open my heart and forgive her. For all these years I was not able to have compassion for what she had experienced. I had not been able to meet her where she was at the time to understand her decisions.

Many people say, 'If I could only go back and know what I know today'. Meaning if, 'I knew then what I know now I would make better decisions' — maybe. You just can't know for sure. What I do know for sure is that when the student is ready, the teacher appears, but NOT UNTIL THEN.

In *The 15 Invaluable Laws of Growth*, Chapter 8, The Law of Pain, opens with a quote from John Maxwell that says, "Every problem introduces a person to himself." I believe that to be true. If I had not been introduced to personal growth, I would not have had the capacity to open my heart to forgiveness for the emotions that I was holding inside. I would not have the maturity to see my life with a new perspective for the first time. I know one of the main reasons that my heart connects to John Maxwell's personal development and leadership is that his material is inspired by his father, Melvin Maxwell. Melvin was a traveling minister who taught through biblical principles. It was shared with me that during the mid 1940s, Melvin preached with my great grandfather at our family tabernacle, The Evangelistic Center, in Indianapolis, IN.

The other idea that I connected to in this chapter on the Law of Pain, was, "A bend in the road is not the end of the road unless you fail to make the turn". as I was reflecting, this quote made me realize that I needed to get over myself and grow up. The pain I was feeling with a job loss was nothing like the pain that my mother had gone through in her life. My mom had experienced significant separation from her mother during her childhood, she lost her mother before I was born, and then the loss of a spouse all before she was thirty. Here I was at fifty years old still holding forgiveness back from her. An unforgiving heart is toxic. Forgiveness is the most freeing experience for your soul. My heart grew ten times the day that I grew my capacity to forgive her.

Many people may experience this type of clarity when they go through similar stages in life. I didn't have children, so I can't relate to raising a child through difficult circumstances like my mom. I can only relate it based on my pain, which provided clarity and allowed me to meet my mom where she was for a moment in time. I have more compassion and understanding for her than I had ever been able to in my life. My heart forever changed on that day. I am forever grateful for the sacrifices my mom made for me. I cherish the moments we spend together.

My mom and I have spent the last decade with more compassion and intentional action, creating experiences that we didn't have the capacity to do earlier in our lives. If you follow us on Facebook, we are traveling, volunteering, and now writing books together.

Personal growth has been the biggest catalyst for my momentum. I have learned a very simple approach that has helped me to develop this mindset. I choose to live my life maximizing every moment.

When I am confused or distraught, I use framework questions from *The 15 Invaluable Laws of Growth*, to provide a fresh perspective. Since my first IMC (International Maxwell Certification) I have been studying my growth. I ask myself these simple questions.

1. What are the gaps that are keeping me stuck?

2. What do I need to learn about myself to grow?

3. Do I really know my value?

4. What is the best way to reflect?

5. What discipline do I need to learn to keep growing?

6. What is the best environment for my growth?

7. Do I have a clear plan on where I want to grow?

8. What can this lesson teach me?

9. Who do I want to become?

10. What will help me to be grow beyond my comfort zone?

11. What am I giving up? Is it enough? Is it new?

12. What can I learn?

13. Who can I learn from?

14. How far can I grow?

15. How much impact can I have?

When I started asking myself these questions, I became more intentional in my life. Through this I have become more confident in what I say yes to and more importantly what I say NO to.

These questions have given me the clarity that I need to make better decisions every day.

"Motivation gets you going, and discipline keeps you growing." John Maxwell

I had been talking about an announcement that I wanted to share with my friends on social media on Saturday, April,7, 2018. This just happened to be the day after I was eliminated from my job. The secret wasn't that I was eliminated! The announcement was my husband, Joe, and I had decided that we were going all in. We were signing a contract with the Indianapolis Museum of Art to host our first *Everyday Leaders 50in50 Podcast Leadership Summit*. This event would take place on March 2, 2019, to review and celebrate the first year of the podcast. We had eleven months to dream, create, and plan. Every interview I grew, I learned more about myself, and I was inspired to make a difference in the world. In December 2018, we reached our goal, 50 guests in 50 weeks. My first guest, Kelly Glover, was a high school friend. His personal story and courage inspired me as he was at a crossroads battling cancer. He wanted to educate and be an inspiration to others. His journey can be found #jukemo Just Keep Moving. My fiftieth guest was Mr. Chip Baker, creator of *The Success Chronicles*. Chip has become a phenomenal friend, best-selling author, and mentor over the years.

One moment can suspend time and bring purpose to a lifetime.

Herb Brooks, USA Olympic Men's Hockey Coach, played by Kurt Russell in the Movie *Miracle on Ice,* says, **"Great moments are born from great opportunity".**

I love this quote because it takes me back to when I was seven years old and my mom signed me up to play Ice Hockey at Perry Park in Indianapolis, IN. The registration said boys' and girls' hockey however, I was the *ONLY* girl in the league for over ten years. What this experience taught me is that you can never compare your growth to someone else. When I joined this league, I didn't have any skills, and I didn't look like anyone else. I had a curiosity to learn. I had to learn everything about the game, even how to skate. I challenged myself to stay committed to the process and what I learned was how to think like a strategist. Learning the game of hockey helped me to develop my confidence with people that were not like me and helped me to develop complex problem-solving skills. When you commit to growth, show up curious, and lean into the process, you will learn life lessons that can transform your life. What you don't know, you will learn. This experience helped me become adaptable, build confidence, and catch a vision to see challenges as opportunities in my life. A growth mindset prepares you for opportunities, and those opportunities create great moments.

March 1, 2019, we were pulling the last-minute details together for our first live event, finishing slide decks, picking up speakers from the airport, and preparing for our speaker dinner at the JW Marriott in downtown Indianapolis. I looked at my phone to check on a plane confirmation for one of my speaker's flights. I noticed an email popped up from GoDaddy. GoDaddy is a website domain provider that I had reached out to when I launched my podcast over a year prior. I had inquired about the domain everydayleaders.com. At the time, I was told that this domain had been owned by someone from Australia since 2002.

What you view is what you do. My vision was inspired by my mentor, validated by my actions, and reinforced by my consistent pursuit of personal growth.

My intention was to build a platform and a brand around the name Everyday Leaders, because I could see and feel the energy in helping people to become consistent, confident, courageous leaders every day. This was the heart of Everyday Leaders. Even though I didn't own the domain, I had already caught the vision.

Never underestimate the power of a vision and the momentum of personal growth.

GoDaddy informed me that the domain everydayleaders.com was up for bid. The auction was ending on March 1, 2019, at 11:21 am. So on March 1, 2019, at 11:00 am, we anxiously signed onto the eBay domain auction and bid three rounds before we WON! We WON the domain EverydayLeaders.com at 11:21 am, just 21 hours before our first event. My heart was pounding so loud I thought it would burst out of my body. I was overjoyed as I stepped into the spotlight on the stage of the Deboest Theater at the Indianapolis Museum of Art. I introduced the conference and announced that my brand, my vision that I dreamed about was coming true and that everyone in the audience was a part of something great!

EverydayLeaders.com was officially mine!

This day was the first day of the next chapter of my personal growth. Every chapter of my growth has uncovered lessons that have transformed my life.

When the student is ready, the teacher appears.

In September 2019, prior to my first co-authored book being launched, I was in a very confusing space in my professional career. I owned a medical device company with the confidence that my product suppliers would assist me in securing investors. What I hoped to be a fruitful partnership was one of the biggest mistakes and lessons in my professional life. Who was I kidding opening and self-funding an international medical device company? I struggled because I had untrustworthy partners. I didn't have the bandwidth to sustain my vision and passion to be able to serve others like I wanted. Gaining clarity from my mentor was what I needed the most as I moved through these challenging times. One afternoon, I was inspired listening to a daily leadership teaching video from John Maxwell. The word of the day was challenge. The message was, 'If you are looking for wisdom, clarity, and courage in your life, read the Book of Proverbs for thirty-one days'. Oct 1, 2019 was the day that I invited others to join me on my spiritual growth journey. I needed to fill my cup and gain clarity and purpose every day. I knew I needed accountability. We started building a community online. Through the years, these thirty minutes every morning have become the foundation for my commitment to personal growth. This one challenge gave me permission to take action and gain the clarity and momentum in my life to build a business and a life with purpose. We meet every day at 7:30 a.m. Everyone is welcome. www.everydayleaders.com

When you are always preparing, you are always prepared.

In May 2022, I was attending a women's luncheon in Delphi, Indiana. We were going to meet the first lady of Indiana, Janet Holcomb. Janet was going to be the keynote speaker and was going to speak on Living a Life with Passion. My friend Deb and I were driving to the event when my phone rang. It was Julia, the event host. She said, how are you? I wanted to call you because Janet Holcomb is sick, and I'd like for you to step in as our keynote speaker today. I was electrified as I hung up the phone. I looked at Deb, who was driving the car. I said, "Ok. Here we go! I'm going to deliver a keynote on Living Your

Passion today."

I encourage you to connect the dots in your life and reflect on the moments that have helped you to gain clarity, build confidence and become courageous overcoming obstacles. If you are stuck, here's my advice: Find a growth minded community and develop a consistent process for personal growth, it will change your life.

What I am learning is it's not what you do in a day. It's what you do every day that makes the most impact, and that will inspire others to become the best version of themselves.

MEET JOYCE BROWN

Joyce Brown is a retired nurse who resides in Greenwood, Indiana with her husband Jerry who is a retired educator. She has one daughter, Melahni Qualls Ake and son in law Joe Ake who also live on the southside of Indianapolis.

She enjoys traveling with family and friends, crossword puzzles, pickleball, hiking and volunteering with various community and church activities.

THE WAY IT WAS

By: Joyce Brown

Before I begin this chapter, I want to extend my heartfelt gratitude to my daughter, Melahni, for giving me the opportunity to share my story. Her belief in my writing abilities is a true honor.

My earliest memory of a life-altering moment traces back to 1953 when my family made the move from Royal Oak, Michigan, to Palmetto, Florida. I was just ten years old at the time.

The decision to relocate stemmed from my father, Karl, taking over his father's grocery store in Michigan. With the rise of big chain supermarkets, my father felt it was time to sell the family business. We had visited my grandfather in Bradenton, Florida, several times before the move, planting the seeds of familiarity with our new home.

Yet, despite some prior exposure, the transition to Florida was far from seamless. I experienced what could only be described as a culture shock. Accustomed to a different academic pace and environment, I struggled to find my footing among classmates who seemed worlds apart from those I had known.

The differences extended beyond the classroom. Our cousins would visit us often to remind me of our vast differences in simple pleasures like sharing the latest music hits or enjoying a slice of pizza which were foreign concepts to us, highlighting the stark contrast between our old and new homes. Moreover, encountering segregated bathrooms in larger towns was a stark reminder of the racial divides still prevalent in the era. Despite the challenges, my family held no prejudices.

The sudden upheaval took its toll, particularly on my mother, Marion. She tried to block out her traumatic life experiences before marrying my father. Her own tumultuous past, marked by familial loss and hardship, cast a shadow over our new beginning in Florida. My mother was often triggered with emotional pain. She did not recall many of the details as we transitioned to our new home due the recent death of her father and leaving all that she knew behind. After moving to Palmetto, my father realized she was losing touch with reality and needed clinical help. She was admitted to a mental hospital in Tampa where she underwent shock treatments to treat her nervous breakdown. Shock treatments were one of the only clinical tools available at the time to erase past traumatic events.

Amidst my mother's struggles, my father embarked on a career shift, transitioning from a butcher to an insurance agent. His knack for connecting with people propelled him forward, leading to promotions and relocations to Sarasota, Fort Lauderdale, and Mt. Dora.

The constant moves tested our resilience, but I adapted as best as I could, navigating through numerous transitions. However, tragedy struck again when my mother's mental health deteriorated, prompting another upheaval in our lives.

Throughout these tumultuous times, I found solace in the steady rhythm of life, pursuing my education, and eventually entering nursing school in Miami. The move to Mt. Dora brought new opportunities, but also deepened our family's struggles as my mother's condition worsened.

During personal turmoil, I moved in with three other nurses in a four unit building in Orlando and worked at Orange Memorial Hospital. Orlando was a very safe community in 1963, where no one locked their doors and I felt comfortable walking a few blocks home at the end of my evening shift.

My mother's episodes of depression became more frequent while she lived in Mt. Dora. One day she went to a neighbor and told them that my father was trying to poison her. My roommate whose mother was also being treated for depression and I traveled to Mt. Dora to see her after my father called me about her condition. We discovered that her conditioned has worsened. My father reached out to the psychologist my roommate had recommended. After an evaluation they started treating my mother with tranquilizers which were limited at the time. She had complications due to her lengthy treatment plan.

My father's work intensified. He found himself unsatisfied with his new work responsibilities and increasing life pressures. He thought the best solution for him would be to move from a management role back into an agent role where he thrived. This move also required another relocation from Mt. Dora to Sarasota.

During this time is where I found love in unexpected places. While I was working at Orange Memorial Hospital, I dated a patient named Benny Bryant. My friend and I ended up double-dating with a friend of his, John. One night we went on a double date and while my friend and I were in the restroom, the guys switched seats and the rest is history. My relationship with John blossomed amidst uncertainty, offering a glimmer of hope amid life's storms.

Before John and I eventually married in 1967, my mother had another nervous breakdown and was committed to the state hospital for further shock treatments. She was eventually released and went back to reside in Sarasota. She committed suicide in 1967 a few days before Mother's Day just before her forty ninth birthday. She had a premonition and had told my father that she was going to die at forty-nine like her mother before her. John and I were married that year, and I was pregnant with Melahni. I always felt sad that my mother never knew that she was going to be a grandmother and I wondered if that would have changed anything. I honored her by giving my daughter her middle name. After Melahni was born, my husband's parents suggested we move to Indiana where I could work in their family nursing home, The Evangelistic Center.

I enjoyed getting back to the mid-west and the four seasons that I was familiar with from Michigan. Even though there was tremendous support from family and living rent free on the nursing home property, I felt trapped. I was working night shift and trying to take care of a new baby. I confided in my doctor, and he advised me to make changes in my life. I took a job at a local hospital working evenings.

We rented a house and John was able to get a job and we thought things were looking up.

Several years into our marriage fate had more challenges in store. John started complaining of pain in his sternum area and after the pain intensified, he was ordered a bronchoscopy procedure. The only relief he had was when he received morphine during his preoperative procedure. A few months later he was admitted to the hospital for breathing problems. They put in a chest tube and tested the fluid in his lungs which resulted in a cancer diagnosis. The chest surgeon said he would not operate on him. John was only twenty-nine years old at the time.

The day after his diagnosis we were on a plane to California. His older brother David had been previously diagnosed and cured from non-Hodgkin's lymphoma at Stanford University. I took my first of two leaves of absences from the hospital in February 1973, Melahni was five at the time we left Indianapolis.

Once we arrived at Stanford, Dr. Rogaway, told us that John did not have the same type of cancer as his brother David. They could never pinpoint the primary site even though it had shown up in his lungs. They treated him with the chemotherapy that was available at the time. This was not targeted therapy like today's medicine with stem cells, T-cells or bio markers. During his therapy we rented an apartment in Menlo Park. After several weeks he improved enough that we returned home to Indianapolis. In just a few months we found ourselves back in California searching for answers. We were there longer than expected and it was time for Melahni to start school, so we enrolled her in kindergarten in Menlo Park.

John was afraid of hospitals and requested me to stay with him whenever he was hospitalized. I would sleep in the chair in his room. His mom would bring Melahni to the window, and he would wave to her through the window, so she knew he was ok.

He ended up having to have a blood transfusion due to all the chemotherapy treatments. They told us he was not responding so they gave us a choice of staying there or sending us home. As a nurse I understood what they were advising us was not going to change the outcome. John's parents begged me to come to Florida to start the recommended treatment plan. They insisted on having John finish his final treatments so he could be buried in the family cemetery in Orlando. We moved the family to Florida, and I enrolled Melahni in her second kindergarten.

John settled into the family room at his parents' house and spent most of his time in the recliner. It was one of the only ways he could relax and be pain free. Melahni loved her dad, and she would get up every morning and run into the family room to check on him. John died in the middle of the night on December 15, and I didn't have the strength to tell her. That morning I asked John's identical twin brother Jim to tell her the news.

In January of 1974, I returned to Indianapolis to the stability of my job at the hospital and Melahni started her third kindergarten. I didn't have any immediate family to rely on, so we built a new way of life together.

The worst thing about returning to work was that I knew I'd get asked how John was because not everyone knew he had passed away. I didn't want anyone to feel sorry for me. It was during that time when the "I am woman, hear me roar" and women's liberation were coming of age and divorces were the "in-thing". I almost wanted to tell people I was divorced rather than widowed, especially when I finally started dating again. I wore my wedding ring for quite a while until I felt ready to forge ahead. I didn't know anyone who was a widow at the age of thirty years old. I'm sure there were no support groups for young widows at that time.

One day when Melahni was starting third grade in 1976, she brought home a weekly school flyer for upcoming sign-ups for hockey. As naïve as I was, I thought surely it would be field hockey and she would get exercise, and be on a team, and learn teamwork, etc. Little did I know on the day of sign-ups that they were talking about hockey on the ice!

Melahni had never ice skated in her life, and it was all boys. I signed her up thinking if they even let her play it would be something! We bought everything used from a sale the coach put on each season. They put her on the ice with a chair in front of her to hold onto and eventually removed the chair and put a hockey stick in her hand. Away she went and ended up liking it better than any other sport she later played, which were many. The boys would tease her and picked on her relentlessly, but the other parents always stuck up for her. At first, I thought she might get injured until I saw all the padding she had to put on, plus the helmet and skates. I also think it gave her a lot of socialization skills to be around boys and fathers to see how they interacted, especially since she was an only child.

Melahni was active in many things during the school year. As a single parent, I couldn't afford childcare during the summers, so she went with John's mom and dad to Nazarene church camp meetings. Her grandfather, Paul Qualls was a song evangelist and had a beautiful voice and her grandmother, Mae, would accompany him on the piano.

Looking back, I was always left alone to figure things out, first as a transplanted child whose whole life up until that point was safe and secure. Learning to adjust to a whole new culture and lifestyle, next to the early loss of a beloved parent who I desperately needed at a pivotal point in my life as a new mother, and finally becoming a widow at such a young age with a small child to nurture and raise. I never asked for help from anyone knowing my journey was personal and my own, to carry on and persevere without complaining about it. As the saying goes, "It is what it is."

The journey was marked by heartache and loss, culminating in John's untimely passing. Left to navigate widowhood at a tender age, I leaned on my faith and resilience to forge ahead, determined to provide a stable upbringing for Melahni.

As I reflect on the twists and turns of my journey, I am reminded of the profound strength found in resilience and faith. Though the path may be fraught with challenges, it is through adversity that we discover our truest selves and the resilience to rise above life's storms. I've always believed in things getting better eventually. My strong faith and determination have been my biggest blessing and made me the person I am today.

MEET KELLY EKWURZEL

Kelly Ekwurzel spent her early career in the financial field, first as a stockbroker/principal, Certified Financial Planner and Enrolled Agent with the IRS, before becoming co-owner of a personal-lines insurance agency. During that time, she did financial coaching as well as teaching three of the Certified Financial Planner (CFP) courses.

After retiring from the financial industry, Kelly became a Certified John Maxwell Coach, Speaker and Trainer and enjoys facilitating the Maxwell course, The 15 Invaluable Laws of Growth.

It is her life purpose to help others be the best they can be through her coaching business, Dynamic Clarity Coaching. Kelly enjoys taking adventurous vacations, has ventured to the equator in Ecuador, hiked in the Andes and walked a portion of the Great Wall of China.

Kelly is a two-time breast cancer survivor, first in 2000 and more recently having a double mastectomy. She has overcome numerous challenges in her life with the help of God.

She is a widow and has 5 children, 8 grandchildren and 6 great grandchildren. She lives in Austin, Texas.

IT IS THE LITTLE THINGS

By: Kelly Ekwurzel

My story actually begins a long time before I was born. It was April of 1912, and my grandmother told my grandfather that she would not get on the boat and come back to the United States from Europe because she was pregnant. That was what my gram said. That ship was the Titanic! Three months later she didn't argue, she simply got on the ship, and they came back to America. Two months later my mother was born. My grandmother had fantastic intuition, and she listened to it, and took appropriate action. She always said it was just "a little thing" that made her say no to that first trip. What little things happened in your life to make you the person you are today? I believe we are an accumulation of those little moments when we grow in some way.

Fast forward a few decades, and we find my newly divorced mother managing a motel in a Florida resort beach in the 1950s, when it really wasn't something that many women did. Those are the kind of women that were my first mentors. Mom and Dad had already gotten divorced by then. Mom was a strong woman and taught me many things. I did not know how blessed we were. We had a great place to live, got to meet numerous wonderful people, and I learned to play baseball. But that is a story in itself. The motel on Clearwater Beach, Florida was the one where the Philadelphia Phillies team stayed for spring training. When they came back to the motel in the evening, they would take their children across the street to the park and play ball. I was always asked to come and play too. I think I am probably one of very few women who can honestly say, "I learned how to play baseball playing with the Philadelphia Phillies." Was that a little thing? The team members would probably have said yes. They were simply being kind and including a little 5-year-old girl with the other children. I believe it was a little thing that became a big event in my life. It taught me several things. First, the importance of being included. Second, even celebrities have private lives and are real people. But most importantly, it taught me to be able to meet and talk to a variety of people.

Living in that motel for several years I got to greet anyone who came to our door (with my mother next to me of course) so I met a wide variety of people. Another little thing? Perhaps, but it molded my personality so that I can literally talk to anyone, regardless of their race, ethnicity, religion, or any other background. It prepared me for times like I recently had, traveling alone to a foreign country. I may have traveled alone, but I was far from lonely. I made friends from all over the world. My energy soared as I met new friends, a few of whom will certainly be lifelong friends.

Some would say I have had a hard life, but I say it has been blessed. Have I had struggles? Yes, of course I have, and I have grown because of them.

Some would say that perhaps I shouldn't have even been alive because I've had so many surgeries and thankfully have recovered from all of them. When I was less than two years old, I had my first eye surgery, which allowed me to see well enough to stop tripping over things that weren't there. A few years later I had to wear a patch on one eye in order to make the other one stronger so that I could read and do other things that most children took for granted. Wearing that to school —

wow, children can be cruel! That was one of the biggest challenges when I was a child, because other children made fun of me daily. The doctors didn't have anything fancy or cute to wear back then, it was simply a black patch so of course one of my nicknames in grade school was Pirate. Not exactly the best nickname for a young girl who already felt out of place having tons of freckles and red hair in a school where many were blondes with golden tans.

Somehow, I found the courage and the self-confidence to get through that period of my life when I was being bullied. I didn't know that it was bullying at the time, but when I look back on it, that was in fact what it was. I was very blessed to have a mother who listened, truly listened, and heard what I was saying. I hope that I have inherited that gift from her. Some have told me that I did.

The first major trauma in my young life happened at the age of 13 when my father committed suicide. Once again, the children I went to school with were not kind. Dad had been one of the businessmen in our community, and it became well known that he had killed himself. I wish I could say that I never let that affect me, but it did. Because of bullying over that issue, I got into fights. And again, my mother listened and helped me to understand what was happening and how to make it better for me. She said I could fight people all my life or I could stop caring about what they were saying and choose to be different. She always listened to what I said, even when I was angry, and I was angry a lot.

I remember her saying that I couldn't expect others to stop saying hurtful things, but I could always choose what my reaction would be. *Choice*! That is such a big factor in attitude. It was then and it is now, every day for every one of us. What kind of attitude do you choose first thing in the morning when your eyes open? Are you wide awake and greeting the day with, "Good morning, Lord. Thank You for another day?" Or do you open your eyes groggily and mutter, "Oh my golly, another day"? I learned from Mom that it was my choice to have a good day or not-so-good day. Some would be better than others, and some would be painful, but they were always better with a good attitude.

Some days there was a lesson that would be learned for a lifetime. The summer that I turned 13 was definitely a challenging one since my father passed, but it was also a life-changing one because of an event that happened a few months later.

I had been staying with my grandmother in New Jersey that summer and became good friends with a young girl who lived next door. Her name was Teresa, and she was one of five children born to the most loving couple I have ever met. Her mother was Pennsylvania Dutch, and had beautiful blue-black hair, and the whitest skin you've ever seen. Her father was as black as you can imagine. At that time, interracial marriages were really frowned upon. It must have been very difficult for their family, but I never felt any tension when I was there. Teresa's brothers and sisters ranged from very dark to completely white. They did not look like each other in that respect. Teresa had blonde hair and a beautiful golden skin color. She could have easily passed for a white person. We did everything together that summer, holding hands and skipping along the sidewalk like many 13-year-old girls do, or at least did back then.

Towards the end of summer, it was decided that we would travel together as far as South Carolina where she was going to visit her grandmother for a couple of weeks. Then I would go further on home to Florida. That sounds like an ideal trip for two young girls, doesn't it? But keep in mind that one was white and the other considered black. In the northeast it was more accepted, but not in the deep south. Back then the Greyhound buses did not have restrooms, so we would make pit stops in various cities along the route. We got as far as the North Carolina/South Carolina border, and that was where the two of us decided it was time to go to the restroom. Off we went with me leading, moving towards the white restroom. Integration had not happened yet. As we got closer to the restroom, Teresa said, "I can't go in there." Such a simple thing, and yet she knew that if someone saw her in there and thought she might be considered colored, as the word was used back then, she could be physically harmed. In the words of the day, she knew her place. I didn't. She was simply my friend. She turned to go to the colored restroom, and I said, "I'll come with you." As you've probably figured out already, that was not an acceptable thing to do back then either. So, we went to our separate restrooms and then came out and sat on the platform as she said, "Under God's stars," until the bus was ready to leave again.

You might think that's just a little thing, but it was something that had a tremendous impact on me for the rest of my life. To think that a person would be restricted from something that they do naturally every day simply because of skin color. It has often made me wonder why we do the things we do to each other as human beings.

There are undoubtedly "little things" in your life that have made a big impact. The things that happened that made you the person you are. That incident made me considerably more accepting of everyone, minorities or otherwise. I tend not to think in terms of labels. Do you think, "That person is white, or Asian or black," or do you simply take the person for what he or she is, a human being, doing the best they can considering all the little things that have happened in their lives? Why do humans tend to label themselves and others?

Have you had experiences like I did that made you the person you are today? I would say yes. Not exactly the same, but definitely because of your "little things" you became the person you are now.

When I was in high school, I worked at JC Penney in the Distributive Education program and rotated from one department to another, learning sales, marketing, office work, and stock work. On one unforgettable November day I remember the assistant manager rushing into the stock room and yelling (it was the first time I heard him raise his voice) to turn on the TV. We were all surprised because we were never allowed to watch TV there. It was turned on and we all stood glued to the screen as we heard about President Kennedy being shot and killed. In addition to that bringing my first awareness to politics, I realized that day how fragile life was and how differently we react to trauma. Mr. Baker, the assistant manager, was rattled by the event so much that the generally mild-mannered and professional man yelled and cried. He startled us all. He said it was a moment in history that we would never forget, and he was right.

At one of my first jobs as an adult, I was blessed to receive a choice of Christmas gifts from my employer. He said he would give me cash or pay my way to take the Certified Financial Planner course. Since I have always loved to learn, I chose education. Perhaps that was a little thing also, but it paved the way for me to become a CFP, as well as a stockbroker and principal, an insurance agent, and later an enrolled agent with the IRS. With that knowledge I provided financial planning and coaching to many clients. If my employer had not made that offer, or if I had taken the cash instead of the education, my life could have been very different. I might not have been able to make the level of income I did, and I probably would not have later met the man who was to be my husband. It was a little thing that became a very large blessing in my life. It allowed me to make a much higher level of income than was common for women in the '70s and '80s. But I did have that blessing, and my husband and I moved our family from Florida to Texas a few years later.

I was blessed to have a husband who was always ready to help others. Here is a "little thing" that he did which became a really big thing.

It was Christmas Eve on a very cold and rainy evening, and as we were coming out of the grocery store, he noticed a young woman looking sadly at the flat tire in a puddle on the rear passenger side of her car. Charlie did not hesitate. He immediately walked over and offered to assist her. I put the groceries in our car and came back to realize that she had a little two-year-old girl who was standing on the seat looking out the back window. I talked to the young woman and her daughter while he finished changing the tire, and we went our separate ways without thinking much about the situation. A few weeks later the young woman appeared at our front door. She asked if she could come in and tell us something. She proceeded to tell us that her parents and her boyfriend had all abandoned her and her daughter. She had told herself that morning that she would take her life and the life of her daughter if she did not get a sign that someone cared about her. We had not realized how depressed she was. Because of his kindness, two lives were saved. Was it a little thing? I would say yes, it was just a tire to be changed, but she would say it was much more than that. We showed her that someone, a total stranger, cared enough to help her and her daughter. Many times, we do not know the results of little things that happen, but that does not mean we should stop doing those little things.

Since I have lived in Texas I have been blessed with many friends. One of them was the wife of a radiologist who specialized in mammography. Our business had been growing, and we moved, and I forgot to do breast self-exams for a few months. Then it was time for my annual physical, and a lump was found. Because of our friendship, I was able to get in for a mammogram and biopsy *the same day* that my doctor discovered a lump. That lump turned out to be a very aggressive breast cancer, and a few days later I had my first breast cancer surgery. They removed 13 lymph nodes and a rather large mass. In the following months I was on chemotherapy and then radiation. I lost my hair but gained so much perspective. At the end of those therapies our entire family got together for the first time in over a decade. We had all five of our children and several grandchildren together to celebrate that I was alive. It was the first time in over 15 years that we had all our children together. So even cancer has been a blessing to me and my family. Several of the children had not been talking to each other for various reasons. But for five days they all stayed in the same house again and made memories. We even got professional photographs done. And those renewed relationships stayed strong for many years.

Life got better and better over the next few years. We were able to sell our home at the top market value and move to a new home closer to the youngest of our grandchildren. Seventeen years passed and the cancer returned. This time I was not so lucky, and because of the radiation I had with the first diagnosis I could not have another lumpectomy. The doctors convinced me that my best option for a longer life was a double mastectomy. What they did not know then, and could not have known, was that my body would reject the expanders and I would get an infection on both sides resulting in two additional surgeries. Because of the infections, what started out as a straight-line scar became something that looks like a drunk carved on my chest. It has been painful at times and simple things have gotten more challenging, but I am here to tell this story. You may say that is not a little thing, but I differ in opinion. We get infections all the time and they go away. These just took longer to heal. Much of the healing was emotional rather than physical.

Instead of three weeks down time, it was over three months. My employer at the time gave us a blessing I could not have even hoped for. I never missed a paycheck. Another blessing… Another little thing? This time, I think not. It was a very big blessing.

Because of the path my life has taken I have had the opportunity to be a leader. Some of those opportunities were as a positional leader and others were not. They made me want to learn and that love of learning made me reach out to a woman who helped me find the path of learning that I have been on for the last few years. That path is everyday leadership, and it is one that you can find also.

I challenge you to look at the "little things" in your life that have molded you into the person you have become. We all have them. Are we always aware of them when they happen? I don't believe we are. Sometimes we are lucky enough to realize they are blessings in disguise. Take a moment and journal on the little blessings in your life. It will give you an awareness of the moments that made you the person you have become. Where is your path leading? Are you a leader because of the little things in your life? I believe you are in some areas of your life.

MEET JODI BONDY

Jodi Bondy is a Michigan girl who ended up in Indiana to raise her family with her husband of 42 years, Tim. They have 3 grown and married daughters and 7 grandchildren. Jodi was a first born to her parents and has a younger sister. Her mom and sister still live in Michigan. Jodi loved nature and being outdoors, she was never afraid to tackle a hard problem or get her hands dirty. As a family, they spent much time camping and exploring new places around the state. She was an athlete, in band and in high school became an Emergency Medical Technician (which she is still active with). In her junior year of HS, her parents moved the family to the U.P., this is where she still calls home. College took her to Michigan Tech where she met her husband. They married right after she graduated with a BS in Biology and moved to South Carolina. They started their family in the south but wanted to be closer to home so they relocated to Indiana (somewhere Jodi never wanted to live!) and now that their girls and families are here, she doesn't see them leaving.

Jodi worked in several jobs before deciding to pursue a teaching career. She taught middle and high school science in several different districts, worked at the university level, coached several sports and stayed active as an EMT. As the environment of education was shifting, Jodi decided to venture into the world of entrepreneurship. She had watched both of her parents do this as well and started not one, but two businesses. She owns and runs a retreat house with her husband and she also helps clients modernize their photos and memories into formats so they can preserve them for future generations.

She still finds time to be mom and gramma. She loves getting together with her own family and having fun making new memories. She currently lives in North Salem, west of Indianapolis on 12 acres with Tim.

You can contact Jodi:

Email: info@hoosierphotoorganizer.com

Website: www.hoosierphotoorganizer.com and www.themagnoliamc.com

FaceBook - Jodi L Bondy

Everyday Moments: Lessons that Transform Lives

GIFTS

By: Jodi Bondy

The visual that comes to mind when you hear this word is one of surprise, bright colors, anticipation, and joy. I am pretty sure everyone loves receiving gifts. The disconnect comes when our expectation of what a gift is and the intention of the gift giver do not necessarily line up. My story involves just that and why it took me down a road that was wild and very rugged at times.

I am the oldest of two girls in my family, 20 months separate us. When I was younger, I never felt that I was wanting for anything. As I have gotten older, I have looked back on this and questioned my naivety. Not that I suffered or was treated wrongly; I guess I had been focused on the good and positive that would come from every situation. My sister and I were a year apart in school, and during the summer months, we would actually play school in our basement. We had an entire classroom set up; I was always the teacher, gave out homework and graded it, made her follow the rules. It was a way of life for us.

As we got older and our time became filled with summer jobs, and extracurricular practices, and training, our little school became dormant. I had Girl Scouts, track, band, babysitting, and blueberry picking to fill my time. Many of these activities included my sister as my tagalong. I was not fond of that even though my parents expected it. I was much more outgoing than my sister, so I often felt weighed down and anchored when I wanted to branch out. I loved babysitting and found it odd that my sister never wanted to be a solo sitter, she would only go with me. And then I had to split my money with her (at 50 cents an hour it was not a lot of money, but it was the principle of the idea). And there were rites of passage that I felt took forever to arrive, only to be told, "Your sister is going with you". Why was I not getting to do things by myself? I now see the gift that she was to me.

As I got older, I decided what I was going to do with my career and life — I wanted to be a wildlife biologist and live in Colorado, so I started down that road. I went to college for biology and then found so many other things while away that I wanted to do and experience. I dabbled in many interesting activities and even forged the path to a minor that no one had done before. My advisor asked what classes I wanted to take to reach that goal. I saw myself as a trailblazer, while many others saw me as a rebel. I did not like following the rules, even though I would. I would always look for alternative routes to take so that I felt like I had control over my path.

I graduated with my biology degree — no job, no Colorado — but a wedding to plan and a move from Michigan to South Carolina. I had met my soon-to-be-husband in college. He graduated two years prior to me, and I felt like I was in a holding pattern. I would now be moving to where his job was, because he would be making more money. I saw my dreams fading away, but I convinced myself that this was the journey I was supposed to be on. I lived with my maternal aunt and her family for about a month before the wedding (I had spent many hours here growing up as well with my cousins), and then we headed on our honeymoon to Gatlinburg, with our final destination in Gaffney, South Carolina.

We had no family or friends when we arrived in this little town. Being an outgoing person, I was able to make connections fairly quick, and we now had "adopted" family. We found a church (not hard when there is only one Catholic church), and the people there became my people. I did all the things I thought a wife was supposed to do, based on what I saw my elders do and not do. I found a job in a bank, but it was just that — a job — no satisfaction or real desire to move up the ladder there. For our first anniversary, I asked that my gift be to quit my job. Scary, since I did not have another one lined up. I gave my notice, we went on vacation to visit family in Michigan, and while traveling, got the call to accept a job with a biology background.

We started our family while in South Carolina, which was hard because our parents and siblings were all up north. We wanted to be closer to them. So the job search began. Two years later, we would be moving to Indiana (somewhere I never wanted to live), and we would be expecting our second child as Hoosiers. Although closer to family, it was still a 6- to 10-hour drive, but we again found friends in our new hometown, and settled in to rebuilding our foundation.

I had been bouncing around in jobs that I thought I wanted, but they still were missing something. I was working in an environmental-related research facility, but since I had young children, I was not able to do fieldwork like the other technicians, so I was stuck in the lab. This was difficult for me. because my outgoing personality was now begging for interaction; most of my colleagues were comfortable working alone. I was so happy when I was able to hire a student lab assistant. However, I was still longing for something new. Since I was working on a college campus, I decided to go back to school. My choices were pharmacy and teaching. I told myself, "I do not want to teach!". And I believed it, but deep down wondered why I played school all those years. Well, I ended up enrolling in secondary education classes to become a science teacher. If I couldn't do the science myself, I could train others to do it. I loved learning while being a wife, mom, and working full time. I was knocking it out of the park with my grades, and I was even thrown into the teaching world when the professor I was assisting went in for emergency surgery and I had to teach a freshman chemistry lab! Talk about being unprepared. But that was another gift I now recognize.

I finished my academic program and left the research world for the education of young minds. I *loved* what I was doing. I had finally found my passion. Don't get me wrong, I had plenty of, "Why am I doing this?" moments, but then a student's light bulb would turn on. I would pour my heart into my classroom, all the time trying not to forget I now had three daughters at home who needed me and my attention, a husband who was still working and providing for us.

I was the only female Science or Math teacher for several years, but I did not let that stop me. I had been down this path before and was used to picking up the slack and accepting the challenges of being out of my comfort zone. I taught, coached, parented, volunteered, and poured myself into all of those around me, helping them to become the best versions of themselves. At the time I did not see it as a problem that I was ignoring myself. I saw myself as a conduit for many of these young people to move into what their dreams were, and I was happy with that.

Then I decided to finally do something for myself and enrolled in classes to pursue a master's degree. I took a one-year sabbatical from teaching for this. I planned to return to the classroom, however, my position was no longer going to be the science teacher; I would be supervising in-school suspension all day, every day. I decided to look elsewhere and then for several years, bounced around in the education world. University, private school, public school, but something was still missing. I finally decided to leave education in 2007, as I had the opportunity to watch my grandson while my daughter started her career. I was also getting to the point that I was not happy with where education was going, and I did not want to hate what I loved. So, gramma daycare is where I landed. This was another gift.

As my focus in my life was shifting from active mothering to occasional grandparenting, I found there to be "gaps" in my woven life. I was having a shift in my identity as far as where my time and energy needed to be focused. I started to question what my purpose was. I kept busy, bounced between activities, looking for my place to make a difference. Family was still very important during this time, but I needed to learn how to loosen the reins so that they could grow into their own people. Several years passed with me floating around like a bubble blown out of a child's wand; no real purpose that I could nail down, although I felt like I was helping others when needed.

The change started in 2014, when I decided to venture out on my own and create my entrepreneurial path. Not just one business, but two. I was feeling reenergized with my love to create new paths and explore areas that were new to me. I had the assistance of colleagues in the business, but again, I wanted to find my way of doing things. I was growing my client base, learning new technology, and adding new skills, but I really did not have the tools for what was required to *be* a business owner. How to honor myself and also convey that to my clients. I had the opportunity to join a Masterclass with fellow photo managers, and we spent time learning about the issues that might be holding us back in our business, how to develop our brand, and expand our reach to the population we were targeting. I learned I was not the only one struggling with these things, but then I also learned that so many of those stories from my past were contributing to this. I was starting to see correlations but needed some help to darken the lines and then own them.

I had the wonderful opportunity to reconnect with a former ice hockey teammate and friend who was also a female entrepreneur and a growth coach (and the reason I am sharing my story, Melahni Ake), I took a huge leap of faith and I hired her to guide me through the *15 Laws of Invaluable Growth* by John Maxwell. I had never spent money on myself without much thought, and this was hard for me because I felt I would have a hard time justifying it to my husband. But I did it anyway.

Working through the chapters of the *15 Laws* and then looking for connections, I began to uncover a treasure chest of gifts. So many of the stories that had been a part of my life were now allowing me to see why I went through them. It may have been years between the source and the outcome, but they were there. I had learned to forge my way through life so that I could again tackle this new journey as an entrepreneur and empty nester. Now, I am not going to say it was all peaches and cream; some of this stuff I was uncovering was scary. I had been living my life as others wanted me to for so long that I had forgotten who I was. I was afraid I might not fit into the life I was living. But I had worked so hard at it while it was happening, what if it was just a façade? That kept me tossing and turning for many a night. I pushed through, and I then realized that I was looking at it from the wrong direction and that I needed to focus on the deep-rooted principles I had been taught so long ago.

There were so many a-ha moments as I studied my growth journey. I began to feel like the skin I had on really was mine. I did not have the doubts in myself like I did midterm in my life. And then I experienced the flood gates opening and the writing on the wall was so big and bold. I finally felt complete. Mel introduced me to the work of Simon Sinek and to the *WHY Institute*. She had recently started offering training on the WHY, so I took another leap of faith. I found out that my WHY is MAKE SENSE. This caused so many lightbulbs to go off for me. I always have an answer, options, possibilities to offer others when they are faced with a problem. Nothing is outside of my scope of trying to figure it out. Now this did tick some folks off, and I often came across as conceited, but I was not trying to upstage anyone, my brain just worked that way. I was/am/will always be a problem solver.

My parents had given me that gift of solving problems when I was growing up. I loved a challenge. I did not always approach it the conventional way that others might — I looked from a very creative, outside-the-box angle. This was revealed to me during a biology teacher conference when I was the only person in the room that had my learning style. I was different and I needed to embrace that.

Once you learn your WHY, you then follow that up with your HOW and WHAT. My HOW is CLARIFY and my WHAT is BETTER WAY. So here I was facing "a problem" and I would ask all kinds of questions to make sure I was clear on the issue so that I could provide the options to reach a resolution. What a magical moment for me — to finally have validation that I was not an impostor, a follower, or "just a girl". I had worth and value that I had never felt comfortable accepting. All my life stories and gifts were in my heart, they pulsed through my body and mind just like the blood that keeps me going every day physically. If you had seen me in those first few days after discovering my WHY, HOW, and WHAT, you might have wondered what I had taken! I was on fire because it was all coming together, and I was now owning my story.

Daily conversations often contain the words "make sense" and I have to smile to myself, "Yes Jodi, that is what you do." I must become more intentional when I offer my ideas to someone else when they are facing a dilemma, because they don't necessarily want me to help. Beyond that I am also realizing that I am so fortunate to live the life I have. The events that happened in my life were all gifts placed there for me to learn from. Granted, some brought me grief and obstacles as they were occurring, but lessons were learned and now when I face a similar situation, I can rely on the knowledge stored in my brain on how to handle it currently.

Being intentional and authentic daily is what I strive for. With my newfound clarity I find this so much easier. I do respect and honor those people who were guiding me early in my life; I am sure I caused a few cases of heartburn and heartache for them at the time. I embrace the gifts I was given now and continue to make connections between my past life and that which I am still building. Being honest with myself has become a more consistent practice. Being available to others is still a huge part of my heart and I will continue to volunteer in my community as long as possible. Being a role model was demonstrated to me as a young person and now I can pass that on to others I encounter. That is a gift in itself. I am sure I rebelled because of immaturity and bullheaded stubbornness. I also know I saw those same attributes from the young people I raised, taught, and coached. I have learned to accept that as normal. I welcome the chance to pass on my knowledge and realize those receiving it will use what they can. Down the road, they may revisit it and see the gift that was given to them as well.

Lifelong learning has always been a passion of mine. I am so very thankful that I had the courage to take a leap of faith to grow more. My story contains so many gifts that were not acknowledged and for that I am sad; I have tried to be better at recognizing the gift giver and will continue to honor them with my life and the things that I do. I am forever humble and grateful to those whose paths have crossed mine and I pray that I continue to carry out my mission on this earth. My story was written long ago, but I am just now unfolding the pages of what will come. May I continue to be a good student, face trials with grace, accept assistance, and love what I do. Gifts should not be expected but received with gratitude and appreciation. May I remain a humble receiver of gifts and an authentic giver of gifts

MEET SHAUNA SNYDER

Shauna was born and raised in Bloomington, Indiana in 1974, and still resides there to this day. She is a Hoosier through and through, although she and her husband love to travel as often as possible. Shauna has worked in the fields of law, insurance, and real estate. Real estate has been a passion shared by her and her brother and became a family career path for many years. The family all worked together for five years in real estate, renovation and design in the San Francisco Bay Area.

Shauna currently works as a Regional Director for Weichert Real Estate Affiliates, where she is enjoying her love of coaching, speaking and training. She has become passionate about growth, and learning, and making a difference in this world, and as many lives as possible. Coaching, training, and motivating others on their journey is something that drives Shauna.

Shauna's greatest desire in life is to help others overcome pain, and those things holding them back, to live their best life, and most importantly to find joy. Shauna is a certified coach, speaker and trainer with the Maxwell Leadership Team. Shauna is married to her husband, Chad, has two bonus children, Cale and Alexa, and her **cherished** grand-daughter, Emersyn. She is a wife, daughter, bonus mom, Gigi, author, sister, and cheerleader to many.

You can find her at www.journeyonyourself.com.

Facebook : https://www.facebook.com/shauna.j.snyder/

Instagram: https://www.instagram.com/shaunajsnyder/

Email: shaunajoysnyder@gmail.com

FINDING *JOY* IN THE IMPOSSIBLE

By: Shauna Snyder

Can I ask you a serious question? Have you lost your joy? Do you feel like you're enough? Has the life been sucked out of you? Do you feel alone? Do you feel stuck? Have you ever been abused, dealt with eating disorders, infertility, or blended families? Both of my hands are up right now. I have answered yes to every single one of those questions. If you answered yes to any or all of those questions, listen to me. I'm just a girl from the Midwest with no college education or formal writing skills. "What does she know?", you might ask. I know you're not alone. Even though you feel it. I've been there. I know you can find your joy again. I did! I know you can heal, and hear me, grow, and thrive beyond your wildest dreams because I did! I am just an ordinary girl, like anybody else, who somehow always felt life had more to offer and never settled. I am just an ordinary girl who has had some trauma. God always gave me the strength to not let it define me and to fight through to find my joy.

One morning as I got up and was doing my morning routine, something said to me, 'Write about your story'. I thought about it for a minute but told myself my story wasn't different from a lot of people's stories. Who wants to hear my story? Some people have had way worse traumas in their lives. I went out to the garage to work out.

I kept feeling something say, 'Tell your story. Somebody needs to hear it'. I am a firm believer in listening. For me, I know it's God leading me, or giving me these gut feelings. You may call it something else. I couldn't fight the feeling I was having.

Let me preface this by saying, this is only my story. I am not a victim. I am not looking for sympathy or for you to feel sorry for me. I refuse to be a victim! I'm not living there! I am blessed beyond measure! I have always felt that the only way I could make any sense out of pain or trauma was to help somebody else. If I help one person today, then I have fulfilled my goal. To be perfectly honest, I once had a preacher stand before me, point his finger in my face, and tell me, "There is a purpose to your pain". This was about halfway through some of the things I have gone through. I have held onto the promise for years! Have you had a promise in your life that you can hold onto?

My story is filled with a traumatic childhood due to undiagnosed mental illness within the family: Marriage, abuse, divorce, infertility, and the trials of a blended family. The stories I will share aren't always pretty, but I can't change any of it. I'm going to share with you some struggles that have come to my life. I want you to see that life can knock you down, can punch you in the gut, take your peace, and try to permanently steal your joy, but we don't have to let it. My mom has told me my entire life — no — she's begged me, to always get better and not bitter. I hope you choose to get better and not bitter. Life is too short to live that way.

Let me begin by telling you a bit about my childhood. This might explain some things you will read. I was raised in a home with quite a bit of struggle and emotional turmoil. We were provided for and well. We had a nice home, clothes we needed, food, electricity, etc. We had those essentials. What we didn't have was the example of a stable marriage. What we didn't have was the example of what a husband should look like. My mom tried. She did the best she could to be both parents. It was always her, my brother, and me. We were alone at church and alone at family functions a lot. Mom was always sitting alone during school functions. I would watch her and could see in her eyes how alone she felt. My dad was gone a lot. When he was home, he was always mad, yelling, and never truly happy. We all walked around on pins and needles to never set him off. He knew how to work hard; he liked nice things and he worked hard for them. My brother and I are both extremely hard workers like him. For that, I'm so thankful. What he didn't know how to be was a caring father and husband. I know he never had an example of that. I'm sure he thought he was doing the best he knew how. I try to give him the benefit of the doubt. Aren't we all just trying to do the best we can? He tried in his own way. I know he did, but he didn't know how to be a dad the way I wanted. It was hard for him to hug me or tell me he loved me.

This trauma in my childhood made me want more than anything to have a real family who did things together. It made me crave attention and love from men. All I wanted to hear was, 'I love you; You're smart; You're amazing,' not stupid like I often heard him say to my mom. I just wanted somebody to love me, who was proud of me, and proud to show me off. I wanted love, and I wanted to be the center of someone's world. I wanted a Hallmark movie! I never got it. I just wanted to be Daddy's Girl. I wanted to see him in the crowd being my biggest cheerleader, telling me how proud of me he was. I wanted him to be my dad and be the man who always protected me. As I sit typing this, reliving some sad memories, I can now see how this has shaped so many things I have done in my adult life.

My father passed away on November 30, 2021. It was sudden. We didn't have a chance to say goodbye, and we didn't have time to mend some fences. At times, it has been tough, but strangely, I often feel my dad close to me. Ironically, in death, my father has taught me so much about love. So much about self-love. I realize I am so much stronger than I ever knew. I have been able to heal from the trauma I grew up in, with grace, and patience, and much forgiveness. I believe without forgiveness it is very tough to ever experience true joy. It doesn't help your future to hold on to past pain. What we must remember is that forgiveness is for us, not the other person. My dad is gone. Nothing productive will come from me not finding forgiveness in my heart. I have stopped feeling sorry for him and about him, even though he was truly never emotionally there for me. I truly believe my dad wanted to be different, but he couldn't be, and that's so incredibly sad to me. I will be eternally grateful that I know I can be different. I have reached a point in my life where I can now focus on the truly amazing things from my childhood that have made me who I am today. With growth and healing, I see that shaped me into who I am. Yes, it hurt, it was painful, but I am at peace. I'm also at a place where I can see the truly amazing parts of me that are from my dad.

I realized with growth and study that I had some pretty deep co-dependent issues. Due to this, I have not been so lucky in love. This even landed me in an abusive marriage. One with physical, emotional, and verbal abuse. I have also been told some horrible, unimaginable things about myself from men. If you read my book, you read some of those stories. Let me give you the short version here. I was never enough. No matter how hard I tried to remedy every bad thing I was ever told about myself, to some people, it was never enough. I heard things like, 'My legs are huge; My nose is big; My eyes are set back in my head so I must never wear contacts, glasses hide that; I look awful with straight hair', which might come as a shock to many people. Straight hair is natural for me. 'I'm stupid and must never open my mouth; I needed a father. That's what is wrong with me.' Are you getting the picture a little clearer? Is there any shock in what I tell myself when I look in the mirror? People can be so incredibly cruel. They don't realize that a person will fight those voices for a very long time, maybe forever. It becomes difficult to look in the mirror and see anything of any worth with those voices constantly telling you years later that you don't measure up. No matter how many people tell you the opposite, we believe the bad things and forget the good.

Let me share something I have learned through the years. We don't have to be the prettiest person in the room to be amazing! We don't have to be the smartest person in the room to make a difference and change people's lives! We all have gifts! We all have a life to live that is lived with a purpose! Let's stop feeling like we don't measure up, and get out there, and be all we're called to be! Let's start lifting each other up instead of sizing each other up! You have something I need! I have something you need, and this world needs us all! On a side note, stop chasing your self-worth with other people, too. Stop getting into relationships that are unhealthy because you're so insecure and crave attention. We all matter! Realize how great you are, and then the right relationship will come along! The right relationships will come along. One where you each lift the other up, not tear each other down.

I now find myself in my third marriage. Although I married an amazing guy this time, I have at times almost sabotaged this one, too. I was always consumed with feelings of never enough. If my husband wasn't telling me how great I was on the hour, I told myself, 'He thinks you are fat; he thinks you're ugly; he thinks you're crazy'. That's the stupid stuff I told myself. I chose to only see the bad rather than see that he holds me at night, tells me 100 times a day, 'He loves me more', calls me during the day to see how my day is going, and we do everything together like I always wanted. Can you relate? It's kind of like that scene in the movie *Pretty Woman* where Vivian looks at Edward and says the bad stuff is easier to believe. Turns out, so much of that bad stuff was all in my head! I get to choose whether I will let those things said about me define me. Those things say more about the people saying them than me. You know what happened when I finally started loving myself and turning off the voices in my head? I found somebody who loved me for me, for all the good, bad, and ugly, and we appreciate each other! I finally found myself in a healthy marriage.

How did I find joy in the impossible voices of ugliness that were screaming in my head, you might ask? I turned around my horrible self-image, and believe it or not, I am loving myself - larger thighs, four eyes, a little back fat, and all. I am reading, and growing, and focusing on food as a fuel source, and realizing exercise is a gift that not everybody is blessed to receive due to poor health! I am not listening to outer voices and opinions that do not matter. This process has been years in the making! Years of therapy, education, and working on myself. I have had to put so much work into changing my mindset from a fixed mindset to a growth mindset. I highly recommend reading the book *Mindset* by Dr. Carol Dweck. I will tell you though, it did not happen overnight. I have had to be so intentional with my thoughts and especially my words. I promise, if you too put in the work, you too will find the joy, and do what seems to be impossible. You too can truly love yourself and realize that you do measure up! It is possible that you too can know that you are smart, beautiful, and needed in this great big world!

Remember when I wanted that Hallmark movie life? You know that amazing husband, and the 2.2 kids with the white picket fence, and loving home that society says we should have. Well, I have that today, but it doesn't look like the picture I painted in my head, and it didn't come easy. This is the point in my story where I have to tell you I was never able to have a baby, a biological one anyway. I never dreamed I would never be able to have a baby. I came from a large extended family. Everybody had kids. There was no way I wouldn't be able to have one. With each procedure I would go through trying to get pregnant, I was sure that particular procedure would be the one, and I would be pregnant the next month. Each time I would be let down yet again. Nothing worked for me like they said it would. This cut to the very core of my being and screamed at me again, you're not enough. Women were made to do one great thing, have babies. I couldn't do that either. I could be a stepmom and have a huge role in raising another woman's children, but I could never have one of my own. What was wrong with me? How was this even remotely fair? I may never understand the purpose of this pain, but I have found peace over it. I believe that someday, I might understand. I still hold on to that word I received so many years ago when God told me there was a purpose to my pain through that preacher. I'm not going to lie to you, this has been hard for me to find joy in. When I see people discarding their babies and continuing to have babies when they're not raising the ones they have, it's still hard. I would be lying if I told you otherwise.

The only saving grace to this part of my story is my adorable 2 ½ year old granddaughter from my bonus daughter. Emersyn is our whole world. She loves her Papaw and Gigi like no other and brightens up our world. For somebody reading this today who is struggling with infertility and isn't having that baby you have prayed and prayed about, keep praying and keep believing! Listen to this, I was 47 before I had a car seat in my car, baby bed in my house, bought formula, diapers, and baby food. Sometimes those blessings in our life look very different from what we think they should look like when they come to us. Most times, the timing is so far off from what we want, we have to learn patience. The timing doesn't fit with our timeline. That will be hard at times. Don't beat yourself up, show yourself some grace, and do everything in your power to choose joy. A shift in your mindset will change everything with this! Let me stop and say this one thing. If you wanted a baby and never had one, go find somebody to pour into. You will find fulfillment. There is no shortage of people who need more people to love them.

I have spent my entire adult life searching for love and acceptance and for somebody to think I was enough. My pursuit of perfection was never that somebody would see my life on social media and think man, she's got it all. No, my pursuit of perfection was if I am perfect enough, and if I am good enough, or do the right things, they will love me and think I'm awesome! How sad is that! I mean I sound pathetic, but I'm honest. If somebody did not like me, approve of me, or want to be around me, I would spiral into depression. I have spent too many days wondering what I did to people. It would eat me alive.

As you can imagine, feeling this way is not healthy or productive, but I didn't realize how unproductive. I didn't find healthy ways to cope at first. I wanted to avoid these feelings at all costs. I did everything in my power to try to get people to think I was great. I tried to work hard. I tried to do everything for everybody. I tried to look great, and be funny, and have the best smile, and appear to have the confidence that down deep wasn't there. I would do anything to feel acceptance and feel better about myself. I would also eat my pain away or spend too much time feeling sorry for myself! Not only have I almost sabotaged my marriage, but I have sabotaged friendships because I have believed crazy things in my head. Have you ever done that? Have you ever been so insecure that you sabotaged relationships? When I stop and think of all the things I have done to try to find that love and acceptance, it makes me sad and mad, honestly. I should have been looking within myself for those things.

I am here to tell you though, there is some silver lining to my story. I want you to find a silver lining in your story. I was laid off at the beginning of the pandemic. For a few days I spiraled. Even though I understood the economic ramifications of what was going on, I still heard that voice saying, 'You're not enough at work. You didn't work hard enough. You didn't do enough'. Here's what I am learning through everything. Number one, I am enough. God made me as He wanted me. I am enough! Number two, I was made for more! Number three, I am learning to love myself, flaws and all. I am figuring out how to love myself. I'm smart. I can be funny. I love and love hard. I am a good motivator and cheerleader to people. I am organized. I am an amazing wife and stepmom. I am an amazing daughter, and sister, and friend. I am a great cook and entertainer. Have I screwed up? Oh, royally, but that is my story! Will I screw up again? Yes! Will I hurt people? Not intentionally, but probably yes! Will I fail again? Yes! But as Dr. John C. Maxwell says, "If you're going to fail, just fail forward".

There are a few things I hope somebody realizes from hearing my story. Don't fear your past. Don't fear your failures, and all the ugly things about yourself. Get up! Get up, wipe yourself off, grow, and go be you! You have a gift! You have a gift that the world needs! You were made for so much more! Don't be defined by your past. Don't be defined by people's opinions and judgments. They do not matter. Use those things and let them make you stronger. You are enough! That's how much I believe in you. Now go be great! Your story is your story for the calling that you have in your life! What will you do with that? Only you get to decide. Don't be a victim, be a victor.

The idea of finding joy in the impossible started when I felt it was impossible to find joy. I found joy through life's trials and tribulations. Life is hard. Somedays it feels impossible to find your joy. It feels impossible to find joy when you're going through a divorce. It feels impossible to find joy when you can't have that baby you so deeply want. It feels impossible to find joy when things are being said about you that are untrue. It feels impossible to find joy when you lose your job. It feels impossible to find joy when you don't know what the road ahead looks like, when the economy and the world are in the state that it is. It feels impossible to find joy when you are broken, and you can't pick yourself up and go forward. It feels impossible to find joy when it feels like God has forgotten you. It feels lonely. It is depressing. We feel anxiety. Sometimes we even wonder if life is worth it, but please listen to me today. Your life is worth living! Don't stop now! Find your joy! Others have been through what you have and found joy in the midst! I promise you that if I made it, you can, too! My middle name may be Joy, but joy is also my guiding principle in life. Joy is the thing I want guiding the crazy ride of life.

So, are you ready? Let's find some JOY!

**GROW
FORGIVE
HEAL
PRACTICE GRATITUDE
LIVE WITH PURPOSE
HELP OTHERS
FIND JOY**

MEET KRIS MAY

Kris May is a dedicated educator, coach, and advocate for women's sports based in Zionsville, Indiana. With a background in both education and physical therapy, Kris brings a wealth of knowledge and experience to her roles. She began her journey as part of the US Olympic speed skating development team, where she achieved a remarkable 500m pack style National Championship in 1991. Following her skating career, Kris pursued higher education, earning a master's degree in Physical Therapy from Regis University in 1997.

Currently, Kris serves as a full-time Middle school teacher and coach, deeply passionate about encouraging girls to participate in sports, especially hockey. She holds the position of Girls Hockey Director for the Indiana Youth Hockey Association (IYHA) and works with USA Hockey in goalie development for females, directing national team development camps for high school-age girls.

Beyond her professional pursuits, Kris finds joy in her home life, residing with her beloved golden retriever Butter, her daughter's rescue dog Rafi, and three affectionate felines named River, Ripley, and Mia. She is also a proud parent to three resilient young adult children.

While Kris has faced personal challenges, including navigating the upheavals of the COVID-19 pandemic and unexpected adversity, she remains steadfast in her commitment to making a positive impact. Through her own journey and the collective experiences shared within her community, Kris hopes to inspire others to persevere and "right the ship" amidst life's storms.

You can connect with Kris on Facebook at Kris May.

LIFE HAPPENS

By: Kris May

When the other authors in this group asked me to be part of this literary venture, I thought I knew exactly what I wanted to share. Then, as it normally does, life happened. All I want now is to share my story in the hopes that it can help someone in a similar situation who was as confused as I was. As you read the following words, try to think to yourself, 'What would I have done in a similar situation? Do I see red flags in my life? Do I act on them? Is it just easier not to confront? How did that work for me in the end? What would I tell my friend, sibling, or child as far as how to respond? Do I listen to my own advice?' And the final question is, 'Am I unknowingly participating in something that is not helping me move forward, and if so, what do I do about it in order to create change?'

Flashback to the summer of 1994. I had just retired from amateur athletics where my full-time job was attempting to make the 1994 Winter Olympic Speed Skating Team. Spoiler alert: I didn't make the team. I was at my parents' home in Indiana, trying to pick up the pieces after falling in my final race and trying to figure out what was next. I decided to distract myself with a summer sport I had loved all through college, so I signed up to sub on an adult slow-pitch softball team. A teammate on the first team in which I subbed, was a delightful young man who I was attracted to right away. For the next two summers we played on the same team, and eventually, one day he asked me out. We formally met in one of our first games by colliding with each other trying to catch the same fly ball. I remember asking him if he caught it, and he said YES, so no apology was needed. We always joked that he only caught it because he was taller.

We proceeded to date through that second summer, and while I knew after three days that I would marry him, it took him three years. A lot happened over those next three years. The kinds of things that tend to bind people together. For one thing, my wonderful young man, a close friend of ours, and I were all involved in a hit-and-run accident by a drunk teenage driver who then fled the scene. Scary, but no one was seriously hurt. Our close friend was from out of the country, so we had fun showing her the town that summer, all the while growing closer romantically, and we continued to lead our team in competition. We were young, and happy, and having the best summer of our lives, but just when we both felt we had the world by the tail, we got the news that I had gotten into graduate school in Denver. At that point, I think we both knew we were in for the long haul. It wasn't possible for him to follow me, as he was building a house and had a good job in town. We knew I would return, so that meant two and a half years long distance relationship.

People questioned our decision but we never did. We knew we could do it, and we did well. We talked several nights every week, and there were many planned and unplanned visits home by me. Of course I always stayed with him, which we never really told anyone, and we were intimate during that time once I knew in my heart that he was my guy. He was my first and my only. I had waited on purpose. I had waited for him. My wonderful young man asked me to marry him in August of 1997, on top of one of my favorite mountains, after he fought through his fear of heights to get us and the ring to the top. I knew I had my fairy tale.

We married in May of 1998 on a beautiful spring day after days and days of rain. It was like the universe was blessing our wedding. It was truly one of the best days of my life! I went to work at a sports medicine clinic, and he continued his job at his architectural firm. I taught him how to skate and play hockey, and we continued to play ball with a group of close-knit friends. Some of those wonderful friends were originally his, and some of them were originally mine, but in time they all became ours. We continued to work on the house together in anticipation of a family. We agreed on three kids and even started talking about names. We spent lots of time together cooking, building, and playing sports, and I knew I had found my Happy Ever After.

We talked often about kids. Both of us were over 30, so we were anxious to get started. I became pregnant in the fall of 2000, and we had our first that following May. What a wonderful day and a wonderful period of time leading up to her birth. My husband was wonderful with me. He made sure I felt good and ate well, and we had so much fun preparing the nursery. It was probably one of the happiest times of our married life. My husband was also fantastic during delivery. It was long. Twenty-eight hours long! I never had a contraction on my own, and she was already late. Finally, after several rounds of Pitocin, and me giving into an epidural at 14 hours, as well as a fever scare, our beautiful baby girl made her entrance. I remember her dad just repeating over and over, "She's so cute!".

Once we got home, the bliss continued, although it was a little tougher as we worked to finish the house. We also had his dad there every weekend to help build. Don't get me wrong, I loved his dad, it was just tough with a newborn, and breastfeeding, and a house that was still very small. Most of our disagreements were about how to care for the baby at night. My husband was against co-sleeping, which meant I had to walk right by Grandpa sleeping on the pullout couch each time the baby needed me throughout the night. I was also the only one getting up with the baby, which was extremely fatiguing. I told myself it was ok, because my husband was working at both his job, and our house, and I was on summer break from my new career in teaching, and then maternity leave. Unfortunately, those issues would grow.

We did finally finish the house, but not until we hired a construction crew in December of 2001, and the baby and I moved into an apartment at the announcement that they would need to remove the roof. I remember my husband telling me that I couldn't find an apartment at that time of year, and especially on a Sunday. I thought, "Watch me," and we were in an apartment sleeping on the floor that night. That is something my husband loved and hated about me. My whole life, if someone told me I couldn't do something, then I was more determined than ever to get it accomplished. In this instance, my husband gratefully joined us in the apartment the next day.

As we were finishing the house and enjoying apartment living, we found out that we were pregnant with our second! How exciting, but to be honest, I immediately cried at the news. All I could think was how hard I was working with the first, and she was only 10 months old. I worried if I could do it and if this would steal away childhood from our first, but of course it was wonderful to have our second on the way. Unfortunately, the pregnancy was not wonderful, with problem after problem. One of the biggest issues was placenta previa which put me on bed rest for two weeks in a third-floor apartment with a toddler and a dog and my husband away at work all day, but we managed. My husband continued to be attentive and continued to work to get our house done, coming home early most evenings to check on the house and have dinner with us. He and I then enjoyed evening time together after I got the baby down, watching TV, talking, and cuddling unless he had work or house issues to finish. I was still doing the majority of childcare leading up to the birth of our second, but the small three-bedroom apartment made it easy to keep track of and care for our toddler, and my husband was working extra hard to grant my wish of having the house done in time for the arrival of the baby.

We finally moved into our home in October 2002, and our second beautiful girl arrived in November, but not without incident. At birth, she was whisked away to the NICU with me barely even being able to see her with her dad right behind her. We had discussed that he would go wherever she went, and he did just that. She had swallowed meconium at birth and was struggling to breathe on her own. For two days, he wore a track from the NICU to my hospital room. When I finally got to hold her, she was still full of wires and under an incubator hood. The nurses told us we might have to go home without her, but my husband stood by my side and helped me convince our doctors not to let that happen. Thankfully after three and a half days, we were all able to depart the hospital together.

Those next few weeks at home were wonderful. The girls loved each other, and their dad was around a lot to play with the toddler and hold the newborn on his chest. I just loved watching them sleep like that. He consented to a co-sleeper in the bedroom to make it easier on me now that we were in our big two-story house. I continued to ask for more help at night with two very young ones, but he didn't seem to understand what he could do to help. I remember him saying, "It seems silly for both of us to get up," which translated in my head to, "You've got this you don't need me". My first real eye-opener was Thanksgiving when somehow, he convinced me to stay overnight with his parents, an hour and fifteen minutes away with a newborn and a toddler. I resisted, but it was hard for his parents to travel to us, and family was so important to both of us. We talked through a strategy to make breastfeeding easier at their house, and he promised he would help, so away we went. When we got there, Grandpa and Grandma had set up a big Christmas tree for our oldest, and she was definitely impressed!

Everything was great until it came to sleeping. Of course, the baby woke up hungry and also woke up the toddler. I began to follow our plan and woke up their dad to help as promised. He would wake up for a minute and then the next thing I knew, he'd be snoring on the bed again. I tried several times but finally gave up to concentrate on corralling the toddler and quieting the baby. Weird that the main concern seemed to be not to wake up his mom and dad when I would have thought the main concern for everyone would have been feeding the baby, getting the toddler back to sleep, and assisting a person they loved who had just given birth two and a half weeks ago. Instead, I saw a glimpse of my future. I did it all while everyone slept. Warmed the bottle for the baby, who wouldn't latch on, pumped the excess milk, and stored it in the refrigerator (which he got upset about since apparently, I put it where "everyone could see it"), and read to the toddler while feeding the baby. Eventually the girls and I fell asleep on the floor downstairs under the Christmas tree as the toddler was content staring at the lights. I tried to talk it out with my husband on the ride home, but all he could say was, "I can't control when I fall asleep".

My next red flag was our five-year anniversary in 2003. The girls were now one and two. My husband really wanted us to stay with his parents that weekend so he could go hunting with his dad. The only day his dad could hunt was on Saturday of that weekend which was the actual day we got married five years before. Of course, I resisted, but my husband promised we would have a nice dinner before we went (which we did). That was also Mother's Day weekend, and he was very convincing saying it would allow him to see his mom for the holiday. I knew he would be resentful if I did not say yes, so again away we went. I guess everything was fine until that Saturday when I found myself alone with his mom and the kids on what was supposed to be a day to be with my husband. I knew I didn't really have a right to be mad, because I had said yes. I guess I was just mad that he even asked and made me feel selfish if I said no. On the ride home I made it clear never again.

After that, things began to spiral a bit. Hunting weekends became ever more important and on weekdays my husband often came home late and maybe saw the girls for five minutes during bath time if even at all. When he was there, he did not volunteer to help. There was no tucking into bed or reading to them on a consistent basis and it was not for the lack of me asking. Whenever I asked or got upset, he would say, "I need my downtime" or "You guys have your routine". We had our routine because we *had to*! I became increasingly resentful, and he became increasingly detached over the next year. I did go and do things out of the house, and it would always hurt me when I would go somewhere and he would say he, "Had to babysit." I would think, "It's not babysitting. These are your children. It's called being a dad". Lots of times, I would just call my mom to come over so as not to hear that comment, and I just kept moving forward.

In the summer of 2004, everything came to a head. We were traveling to Colorado on vacation, and I was at my wit's end with asking for help and not getting it. I had even shared with my husband an episode that year when I was so tired driving home from working full days and doing everything for the kids during the evening and at night that I fell asleep at a stop light. A beeping car woke me up, and all I could think was, "We are close. Just get them home safely". All I remember after that was feeling so relieved when I pulled into the garage and laid my head back on the headrest once the car was stopped. The next thing I knew, I woke up in the garage, still belted in my seat with the car running, the door down, and the kids asleep in their car seats. Of course, I panicked! I immediately opened the garage door and ripped the kids out of their seats to take them to fresh air.

Thank goodness nothing happened, but it took me two months to get the courage to tell my husband, and he showed no emotion. I actually think he thought I was making it up to make him feel bad. That's when I realized this was my reality. It was not going to get better, so I had to be happy with it or be angry the rest of my life. While on vacation, we took a hike, just he and I, where I found out just how distant he felt. I again asked for help, and he made it clear he was doing all he thought he was capable of. He also shared with me that he had thought about leaving as all he felt from me was anger. He said he was "traditional" and felt his job was to work and provide, and my job was the kids and the house, like his mom. I mentioned the huge difference was that I worked full time outside the home, unlike his mom, and to that he said it was impossible financially for me to stay home. I wasn't asking to not work. I was asking for support in raising our family.

I was appalled at his words, especially his threat to leave. I made it clear that I was in it for the long haul, that I waited for him, that I loved him, that I chose him. I just needed help and that the reality we were living was not what we had agreed to. I reminded him of the talk we had while we were dating, and he was working every weekend. He had no time for me, and I remember saying, "I don't want to marry someone and have them be an absentee dad". I was fully expecting at that moment to break up, and I was stunned when he said, "Maybe I need to work on this". My heart soared as I knew I loved him. Then a short eight years later, here we were having the same discussion, but this time he was saying, "I can't do any more". The reality was he initially did stop working weekends, but over time he just replaced working with other things to distract himself.

Maybe that mountaintop discussion was the moment I began to worry or even realize that his love was conditional, so I decided to meet his conditions. I would stop asking for help. I would do it all, and I would love him for his strengths. I told myself in the grand scheme of things, workaholism wasn't the worst flaw your husband could have. I even convinced myself that maybe I was expecting too much. We also found out on that trip that we were pregnant with our third, which would quickly turn into something that forced us to work as a team.

After all this strife and my husband's disengagement in day-to-day family life, the one thing I always knew and held onto was that he would be there in an emergency to keep us safe and to protect us. We didn't know it yet, but there was an emergency coming our way. During our first ultrasound with the new baby, we were informed that our beautiful little 18-week-old baby boy would likely not make it to term. They found out that he had total organ reversal or Ivemark Syndrome and told us right there that we should consider our options. Despite the advice of our local doctors, we stayed committed to the pregnancy and pursued all testing options, hoping for the best, until we found ourselves with a specialist in Michigan, where further tests revealed major problems with his brain development and the complete absence of major organs. Even the specialists agreed that he would likely not make it to term, which could also be risky to me, and if he did that he could not live outside the womb. In the end, with our help, he was stillborn at the age of 20 weeks. We were able to hold him briefly until he was cremated for him to return home with us.

On the way home, just the thought of telling the two toddlers what happened to "the baby in mommy's tummy" was almost impossible, but my husband was right there supporting me while we were away, just as I expected. Unfortunately, once we arrived home it was back to a familiar pattern. I worked all day, took care of the kids, and cried all night. I begged my husband to go to counseling with me, but he refused over and over. He said, "All they will do is blame me or try to change me and I'm not going to change." He finally did come once, but never again. I didn't want to change anyone. I just needed support, and I thought he did too. I got through the pain of losing our son basically on my own, and after that my reality was clear. My husband was very clear about what he would do and what he would not do, and I was determined to make that work for all of us.

We continued to struggle for a while, but eventually, we got pregnant again with our miracle boy. It wasn't in our plan, but it was clearly in someone else's. Nothing really changed following his birth except our attitudes. I learned not to ask for things I knew were a no-go, and my husband relaxed once he didn't feel so much pressure, I guess. We cruised along happily for a number of years. Me keeping the house and the kids going in addition to my new career as a full-time teacher, and him working, hunting, performing house maintenance and helping with the kids when he felt he had the time. I felt loved and I think he did too despite both of us feeling constantly always exhausted from our separate roles.

As the kids got older and began to get involved in more things it was frustrating for them and for me not to have daddy around at many of our events, but family life felt comfortable. It seemed my husband's self-esteem was being boosted by his incredible work accomplishments and I was very proud of the people my children were becoming.

I remember we would still get in little arguments about him not being there for the kids and he would say, "I would have to miss a million-dollar meeting to come home early". All I could think was, "There are three-million-dollar meetings right here wishing for your attention", but I would try to understand because I had to. I was determined to make things work for him and simultaneously be sure my kids had what they needed in the way of attention, love, and support. He was the love of my life. The person I had chosen in sickness and in health, for richer or for poorer, and to be faithful only to him 'til death do us part. We had made it through building a home, the loss of a child, helping another child navigate autism, disciplinary challenges with the kids, the creation and crash of a business which devastated us financially, the alienation of relatives on both sides of our family, the death of several relatives, and we were still lovingly moving forward together. There was seemingly nothing we couldn't handle, or so I thought.

Then the roof came crashing down in July of 2020. Obviously, it had been building for a while unbeknownst to me. On July 4, 2020, which was the first night of our yearly Colorado vacation at the cabin, my husband stayed up all night after fireworks on his phone. I thought he was working, and I felt bad for him, so in the morning I inquired about what he was doing hoping to encourage him to relax and revive in this beautiful place with two weeks of quality family time ahead of him. Instead of the loving and supportive conversation I expected he informed me that he had been up constructing a 42-item list of all the things he hated about me and proceeded to share it with me. I just sat there in bed beside him silently stunned and trying to process what was happening. Then after he read through all of the items, he told me, "You are a wonderful friend, an amazing mother and a terrible wife". I can't even explain the blindside. Just the day before at the campground I was watching him sleep and thinking how lucky we all were to have each other and just how lucky I was to have found him, and that despite all the challenges life had thrown at us, we had found a way to make it work. Little did I know but that was *not* my reality. He was already plotting his escape.

We proceeded over the next year, "to work on it," which I now think was just an act on his part. I memorized the hate list and tried to address every item, but as time went on all he could say was, "You're making progress but I don't trust you". No matter what I did he pulled further and further away and spent more and more time with his new female workout partner, but they didn't just workout together. He accompanied her to doctor's appointments, performed small mechanical tasks that supposedly her husband wasn't good at, helped her through the death of her father, even spending *full* days helping her clean up his estate, and attending her daughter's volleyball games when he couldn't be bothered to come watch his own kid's games.

He spent increasing amounts of time away from home, but now it clearly wasn't just work. He began to be more and more concerned with his appearance and his clothes. Whitening his teeth and shopping for "non-dad" clothes and shoes. All the while moving further and further away from me physically and emotionally. Of course, I progressively got more and more distraught to the point where it was impossible to hide my feelings. I remember during one argument he said, "I thought I would make you so mad that you would just leave." I had no idea what he meant, because all I wanted to do was figure out how to make things better. He just seemed to want to disengage further. He even said, "I won't talk about it, I won't be your sounding board for our relationship." If not him, then who?

I probably knew then it was over, but I kept beating my head against the wall. One thing he used as leverage to justify his behavior were phrases like, "Why didn't you do these things years ago? Why did I have to go to these lengths to get you to respond?". It became apparent that there was nothing I could do, which was so confusing. This was my husband, the man I loved and supported for 26 years?? I was being blamed for everything. Meanwhile, I had gone over the top to accommodate his needs and wishes for years, even to the detriment of myself. I had watched my kids ache for their dad's attention and proceeded to soften those feelings with excuses like, " He's supporting us by working," and, "He loves you and he's doing his best." The kids and I used to sit around and brainstorm ways we could spend more time with him. Sometimes we were successful, like daddy movie night, and sometimes we were not, like when the girls got him a hat from their hockey team and included a note with a schedule asking him to come watch. He watched one game that season and spent most of the time at that game looking at his phone.

In the end he left. Despite my best efforts, the love of my life, the father of my children, the person who promised to love, honor, and cherish me, had walked out. Clearly, he had his reasons, and I'm sure they seem valid to him, but in my mind, there is no reason good enough to give up on your family. At this point, the kids seem relatively okay. I realize that the limited time they see him now is about as much as they did when he lived with us, so nothing is much different to them. I have made sure that they still have me, their home, their pets, their friends, and their lives as they have always known them.

As for me, I'll get over it because I have to, but I will never understand it. I will never understand what would compel someone to give up on their family and throw away their marriage, especially one built on love. The only thing I can come up with is that maybe it wasn't built on love for him. Maybe he never loved me but was just following my plan. After the hate list he would often say, "You always get what you want". I really never had any idea what he meant, as I know, and my kids know, that all I ever wanted was his love and attention. I wanted us to feel more important to him than everything else including work, and for our family to be his number one priority. All I know now is I did my best.

I always say, "For every adversity there is opportunity," and I know that is true here. For one thing, I have a much better perspective on what actual adversity feels like and what it can drive a person to think and do. Although hard to admit, there were moments when I considered that the world might be better off without me and that simply not being here would be easier than facing the breakup of my family and the loss of someone I loved so deeply. I never would have dreamed I could have such a thought until this situation, but I did! I am forever thankful that multiple people were there to help me through that dark period. Picking up the phone in the middle of the night. Hugging me as I cried. Boosting me up when I was determined to tear myself down and helping to remind me of all that I still had and not what I didn't. I also now understand how someone can be so anxiety ridden that they cannot go to school or work or even get out of bed. There were days that I couldn't eat, or move, or even put cohesive thoughts together.

If you ever find yourself assisting a person contemplating ending their life, JUST BE THERE. Get them to the next safe moment. At that point, there is no reasoning there is just protection by being present. Similarly, when dealing with an anxiety-ridden person just keep supporting and working to get them to the "next right step." Your friend or loved one may get angry with you for suggesting they need help. I did, but don't give up! I'm finally starting to feel like me again, but I never could have gotten here without my kids, my friends, my colleagues, and the relatives that still support me.

The moral of the story is, Life Happens, even when you've done your best, even when you don't deserve it. The question is, how will you respond? Whether you are the person in the situation or a friend, family member, or trusted person trying to help, that simple contemplation can make all the difference for you or the person you are assisting.

As the saying goes, "It takes a village". I am forever thankful to my village, and I will forever pay it forward for them.

MEET SHELLY BAYS

Shelly Bays is a rising author contributing her voice to this collaborative book project. With a background as an entrepreneur, business, and life coach, leadership and communication trainer and keynote speaker with a flair for storytelling, she brings a fresh perspective to the chapter she authors. Her writing reflects her dedication to helping individuals thrive through teaching and coaching from her journey, not from perfection. Shelly enjoys immersing herself in new experiences, traveling to far-off destinations, riding Harleys with her husband, and cherishing moments with loved ones. Currently based in Lafayette, Indiana, Shelly is excited to continue her journey as an author, making a meaningful impact through her words and teachings.

You can contact Shelly here:

LinkedIN: www.linkedin.com/in/shellybays
Website: www.shellybays.com
FaceBook: Shelly Bays Training and Coaching
Instagram: @shellybayscoaching

A FUTURE AND A HOPE

By: Shelly Bays

I am a warrior. I am also a woman, mom, wife, daughter, sister, aunt, and grandma! And I am an entrepreneur; for more than half of my life I've been an entrepreneur, but I sometimes still struggle with feelings of inadequacy, or being "too much," imposter syndrome, etc. Those feelings that stop you in your tracks and make you doubt yourself. We all have these feelings because we are human. We let the little voice inside our head whisper things to us like, "Who are you to think you can (fill in the blank)?" or, "What makes you think you are *worthy* of love, happiness, health, success, etc.?". You get the picture, because you have likely heard those words in your own head. You and I are more alike than different, and one truth that we must accept, if we are to thrive in life, is that those feelings don't have to control us or our life choices, decisions, and direction. It took me years of searching, learning, reflecting, and doing internal work to understand that my past experiences, and the words said to me had shaped how I feel about myself, and why I had made so many of the choices that took me in directions *away* from what I desired instead of *towards* what I wanted to have and do, and more importantly, who I wanted to *be*.

No matter what my circumstances were as a child, teen, or young adult; no matter what bad or good things happened then or happen now, I have the power to choose today how I will respond, how I will move forward, and what that looks like. And so do you!

My guides and mentors have been people like Tony Robbins, Bob Proctor, Brené Brown, Simon Sinek, Malcolm Gladwell. I've studied the greats like Napoleon Hill, Dale Carnegie, James Allen, Earl Nightengale, John C. Maxwell, and Jesus Christ. I've been building my ideal life through personal development since the age of 19. In fact, it started before that because I was a multi-sport athlete in high school who earned a track scholarship to college, and then walked on the volleyball team and earned a varsity spot, so I have been working on self-improvement and personal development for most of my life.

I've immersed myself in neuroscience, Neuro Linguistic Programming (NLP), Positive Psychology, and every personality or behavioral assessment that came into my awareness. I have a hunger for learning, growing, and most importantly to me, understanding. I am so curious about the human experience; that of others and of my own. How do I connect with others in ways that show them that I value them? How do I increase my influence as a leader, and be a person of great character, integrity, and significance in my world?

What I've learned is this: The bottom line, no bullshit. The only thing standing between me and the life that's my ideal, is me. And it's the only thing standing between you and your ideal life too. What are we to do about that? I've had many days of my ideal life, and they include abundances of joy, family, health, wealth, and love! They also include pouring into others, giving back to my community, and overcoming challenges, obstacles, heartache, and pain, as well as adventures, kicking back, roaring forward, and easing off the gas. My ideal life likely looks different than yours. We are each uniquely made for something different with our individual combination of gifts, talents, and strengths. I can't be you, and you can't be me. And that is absolutely the most beautiful thing! Wouldn't it be boring if we were all exactly alike? That realization and the acceptance of it is unimaginably freeing.

You may have heard the saying, "Comparison is the thief of joy." It is the truth. My truth and yours. You can take that one to the bank. Does this mean that we should never compare anything in our lives? I don't think so. What I believe it means is that we should not compare our journey to another's. We shouldn't compare our body to another's. We shouldn't compare our wins and losses or our relationships to another's. We *should* set our own standards and compare ourselves to *them* as we move towards our future with worthy goals and ideals in front of us. And we can minimize the negative impacts of comparison by recognizing and reflecting on how far we have come each day from where we started our journey. We can choose to be *grateful* for what we have had, what we have now, and what we "must have" in the future. You get to decide what those "must haves" are. And they can be different in the future from what they are today. In fact, as we grow, our "must haves" will likely change.

Behavioral science says that human beings have two powerful driving forces in life: fear and pleasure. We make split-second decisions based on avoiding pain (real or imagined) or chasing pleasure (also either real or imagined). Which decisions or paths we *habitually* choose sets us up to either remain in place or move ahead. When we don't understand how and why we are making those choices, we struggle to move ahead, or we go one step forward and three steps back. The good news is, with the amount of research being done in neuro and behavioral science we now know that there are scientific reasons for these habitual choices. Our Reticular Activating System (RAS) and subconscious mind direct our thoughts when we are not actively thinking and being intentional in our decision making. Our subconscious mind is trying to protect us and keep us in what is known and comfortable. And too many times, what is known and comfortable is not good for helping us moving forward. It keeps us stuck, unhappy, worried, and fearful about the future. We end up focusing on what could go wrong instead of what can go right! However, there is another way.

We have been given the gift of *free will*, but so many people don't really exercise it. Have you ever heard someone say things like, "It just wasn't in the cards for me," or "If I didn't have bad luck, I'd have no luck at all?"; how about, "My whole family is poor, and they always have been?". This is a sign of someone resigning themselves to a generational curse! Folks who get caught up in that kind of thinking and verbalize it are unintentionally allowing limiting beliefs to run their life. They are giving up their free will to make different choices. To learn to think and do in a different way that will give them the opportunity that we all deserve as human beings. The opportunity to create our own journey. Instead, so many believe, think, and do what their parents, grandparents, friends, and others in their inner circle do.

It reminds me of the story of the Christmas ham. Maybe you've heard it? It's Christmas morning and the kitchen is bustling with activity and chatter with mom, daughter and grandma preparing the family Christmas dinner. Mom gets the ham from the fridge and the roasting pan out. She lovingly presses in cloves all over the ham in an intricate pattern. And then, she cuts both ends off the ham and places the rest in the roasting pan. The daughter, who is watching the whole process curiously asks her mom, "Why do you cut the ends off the ham?" Mom replies, "That's how my mom did it." The daughter asks Grandma why she cut the ends of the ham off before putting it in the pan. Grandma answers, "That's how my mom did it." The daughter isn't satisfied and still curious, so she goes to get Great-Grandma from the living room. "Great-Grandma, Mom cut the ends of the ham off before she put it in the pan, and when I asked her why, she said that it was because that's how her mom did it. Then I asked Grandma why she cut the ends off, and she said it was because it was how YOU did it. So I'm wondering, why do you cut the ends off the ham?" Great-Grandma looks at her great-granddaughter with a twinkle in her eye and says, "I cut the ends off the ham because I didn't have a bigger pan that the whole thing would fit in." And there you have it my friends — two generations didn't ask why, they just followed suit. The moral of the story is that we can and should question our beliefs and patterns of behavior. It's healthy and it gives us the opportunity to *decide* if a belief or habitual pattern is something that serves us now and will continue to do so into the future. Taking the time to question, reflect, and choose will result in some beliefs being kept and cherished with the bonus of *knowing* that the belief is important to you, serves you in a positive way, and is aligned with your values. And some may have no real basis to continue, because although they may have served us in the past, they do no longer. Some have never served us in a good way. Many of our unquestioned beliefs and patterns are limiting our potential.

Dr. Bruce Lipton, PhD, said in his book *The Biology of Belief* that, "95% of our lives comes from our subconscious programs." That's significant. Some of those subconscious programs run our bodily functions like heartbeat, breathing, muscle movement, etc. Those aren't the ones that I want you to question. I want you to examine the others. The ones that we learned. The ones that we blindly accepted because of where they came from — people we trusted to have our best interests in mind. This could be your parents, grandparents, teachers, friends, religious organizations, etc.

When we were children, our minds were like sponges. We absorbed and accepted without the ability to rationalize and question. This was during the super learning period, ages 0-6, the same time we were learning to crawl, walk, and speak. Then we entered the next development stage and learned how to read, societal rules, family rules, how to ride a bicycle, *and* we were learning so many of the things that are responsible for what we believe about ourselves now. All without the ability to reason, rationalize, compare, and question. Of course, little ones ask lots of questions, but when you think about it, they are most often "why" and they are further related to them being the center of the universe, not questioning the validity and basis of the rules they are learning, and the beliefs being impressed upon their minds.

Each day you can choose your attitude and where to focus your attention. And that, my friend, is truly a gift. Let's not squander it by letting old negative or limiting thoughts, beliefs and habitual patterns rule our present and our future thinking without questioning them. We have a choice! We can transform our results and our lives by living with intention each day, and questioning, reflecting, and rooting out negative and limiting beliefs and replacing them with empowering ones. Does this mean we never backslide or have a bad day? No, because we can't control everything that happens; however, we *can* train our brain to quickly go to a positive state so that we can move through the negative or limiting thoughts and feelings faster, regain clarity, and refocus on what we **can** control: Our thoughts and our responses.

If you're like me, you might find yourself struggling at times with feelings of "imposter syndrome," or being stuck or paralyzed with feelings of fear or anxiety when making decisions about how to move forward. Remember this — you are *not* alone. And one of the top things that I encourage you to do is to develop a strong network of friends and/or family to help you to remember who you are when those feelings come to the surface, as they inevitably will. Nothing that we strive for that is worthy of our efforts comes easy, nor without a battle in our minds.

I want to share the number one way that I have been able to transform my life, and it transforms smaller moments, too. This practice can help you to move forward towards the future you desire, bravely, while feeling happier and more joy-filled in the present.

Before we talk about this powerful transformation tool, I also must talk about one of the most powerful emotions, maybe *the* most powerful, and that is *hope*. Hope for the future, and that the future is good. When we lose hope for the future, we spiral out of control into negative thinking and negative energy. And those thoughts and that energy are a catalyst to knocking us down and holding us there. There is a way to regain hope, and I believe the best and fastest way to build hope is with the intentional practice of *gratitude*. This is the transformation tool of tools. Focusing on things that we are grateful for, especially amid challenge, pain, and disappointment, creates an instant change in our brain chemistry. It releases serotonin and dopamine, the feel-good hormones. It creates a space for regaining clarity and logical thinking. And it's critical for paving a way out of whatever negative emotion and thinking is happening in the moment.

I am not discounting negative emotions like sadness, pain, grief, heartache, and disappointment. In fact, to help us to move through those emotions, we should allow ourselves to feel the emotions that came with the event or situation. If we don't give ourselves permission and space to fully feel, observe, and name the emotions, without self-judgment, and instead bury them, they become unresolved and start piling up. And at some point, they erupt. When that happens, it's not usually pretty. We may also inflict pain and damage on others in our lives. Those you love and care for can become collateral damage to your unresolved feelings. Instead, let's give yourself permission to feel the emotion, observe how it makes your physical body feel, and what thoughts come with the feeling. And — this is so critical — do this with *non-judgement* of yourself. Then you can name the emotion through reflection and take away some of the power of the emotion by reframing it, and then begin moving into a positive state. This is when we use gratitude to speed up the process of moving forward, when our mind is clearer, and we can become intentional in our thinking again.

In my research about cultivating resilience, mindful self-compassion is seen as a key to being able to bounce back from life's challenges. There are many behavioral and neuroscientific studies showing that those who make it a practice of feeling, recognizing, acknowledging, naming, and observing their emotions and then reframing them to move into a positive state has lasting effects. When it was done repeatedly over a period of three weeks, the effects lasted up to a year. With intense and deep emotions, it's not typically a one and done. However, in a moment of anger, or disappointment, or other negative emotion, we can use this strategy or practice to move with extreme speed from negative emotions and thinking into a more positive state.

Dr. Kristen Neff and Dr. Christopher Germer, cofounders of The Center for Mindful Self-Compassion, are my go-tos in this area. I highly recommend their website and learning opportunities from Dr. Neff and Dr. Christopher Germer. You can access their resources and trainings at www.centerformsc.org.

Another key to creating a process or practice of mindful self-compassion is understanding and accepting that we will have challenges, sadness, obstacles, and disappointment in our lives. When we submit ourselves to this understanding, it gives us permission and perspective, not resignation, the freedom to feel, learn, release, grow, and move forward.

The author of *Think and Grow Rich*, Napoleon Hill, once wrote, "I am thankful for the adversities, which have crossed my pathway, for they taught me tolerance, sympathy, self-control, perseverance and some other virtues I might never have known."

This brings me back to the "golden key" of a life filled with every kind of success: Gratitude. Practicing gratitude can be a quick hit when you are feeling overwhelmed, sad, disappointed, etc. to get us out of the spiral of negative and foggy thinking, and when practiced consistently, over time, it allows us to be predominantly in a mindset that is more positive and clearer, which in turn allows us to tackle the hard stuff like rooting out limiting or self-sabotaging beliefs and habits, questioning them, and then either kicking them to the mental curb, or shoring up the ones that support us in being who we desire to be, because who we *believe* we are determines what we will have and do. It promotes and supports feelings of "hope for the future."

I am so invested in the fact that I have a future and that it is good (fully understanding that there will be challenges, obstacles, and hard days as part of that future and the journey to it) that I had the words "Jeremiah 29:11" tattooed on my right shoulder blade overarching a cross that I designed. I'm not suggesting you go get a tattoo, but if you are into ink, it's a great visual reminder for me. If you are a Christian and haven't read that scripture, it's powerful. I also know the context surrounding it, but it is the power of knowing that I have a future and a hope that is a guiding light in my life. For those who aren't familiar with the scripture, or aren't a believer in the Christian faith, let me share it with you. This is from the ESV (English Standard Version) of the Bible. Jeremiah 29:11: *"For I know the plans I have for you, declares the Lord, plans for welfare and not for evil, to give you a future and a hope."* I don't know about you, but that scripture is something I can hold on to no matter what my current circumstances are, or what situations are occurring in my life. And it is an *active* and current statement of God's Intentions for my life. This isn't just something He declared in the past — it is an active and ongoing statement for each of us living now, and all who will be born in the future. That means to me that I can count on this active statement of hope for me, my children, my grandchildren, and generations to come. Those words and knowing the truth behind them is what I have held on to many days in my life, and they have transformed my mind, my journey, and my choice to live an intentional life.

Hope and gratitude are intertwined. It is difficult to have one without the other. If I have hope, I will be grateful. If I practice gratitude, I will find hope.

I encourage you to not make this a difficult practice. And whether you are in a "good" place in life today or not, beginning or getting back into a habit of practicing gratitude daily will transform your life —one day, one hour, one moment at a time.

Here are some of my favorite ways to practice gratitude:

- First thought – I start my day with this. When I wake up, my eyes pop open and I look up and I tell my Heavenly Father *"Thank You for another day not promised."* I am incredibly grateful for just waking up. If you are not a believer in God, maybe you are speaking to the Universe, or whatever Higher Power you do believe in. I have been doing this for years, and I very much believe that it is the answer to the question my husband asks me all the time, "How can you always be so happy in the morning?" It's because I am grateful to have been given another day here on earth with him, and all the people I may be able to have a positive impact on.
- Gratitude journal – Writing and speaking, each day, 10 things that you are grateful for does a couple of things for us. It is a way to express gratitude using more than one sense. It is a practice of using our voice to verbalize, our hands to write to anchor in those thoughts more deeply. It is also a record for us to go back to on the hard days when we are struggling to find things to be grateful for.
- Gratitude index cards – To be written down and carried with us so that we have a stream of things that we are grateful for to go to when we recognize we are starting to think negatively and want to quickly disrupt that pattern, or need to get out of a funk, or are struggling with negative emotions and thoughts

about ourselves or others. Pick a few and say them out loud, repeating as necessary until you begin to feel the change of your emotions, your body relax, etc. Be aware of how you are feeling as you focus on and speak your gratitude.

- Gratitude sticky notes – I like to put sticky notes in places where I will find them later, like on the back of a door that I don't open frequently. It's a little surprise, and when I open that door and see it, I grin. Other great places are on my bathroom mirror, my car sun visor, etc. Places I can get a reminder or quick gratitude hit. The visor sticky note has helped me to *not* get road rage more than a few times!
- Gratitude letters – Writing letters to those in your life who you are grateful for and explaining *why* you are grateful for them in your life. Be specific. I'll give you an example with some background: My mother was very physically and verbally abusive to me when I was a child. I love my mother very much. She is one of my best friends today. She was only 16 when I was born, and had some generational beliefs that were not helpful to being a mother who was in control of her anger, emotions, frustrations, etc. However, after I moved away from home and started working on my own personal development, I realized that she was only behaving in ways that she had been subjected to and had been modeled to her. She was doing the best she could with what she knew. And my mother also came to realize that how she had parented was more often harsh and damaging, and she owned it. She apologized. I had already forgiven her years before the apology and was already grateful for many things about my mom. My mom is courageous—she was a 16-year-old high school junior when she got married and had her first baby, me. She went back to complete her high school education through obtaining a GED when she was in her 20s, after she had my youngest sister in 1969. She is gifted in ways that I am not and has been a great advisor in my life. I could go on and on, but I think you get the message. Find

specific things to be grateful for about the person or your relationship and tell them. Write it out on a notecard, stationery, or notebook paper, but do it and send it. Handwritten is the best in my opinion. I love receiving handwritten notes and letters. It is special, and for me is a demonstration of the depth of the feelings from whomever I receive that handwritten note, letter, or card from. It takes additional work to handwrite a note, address an envelope, get a stamp, and get it in the mail. I will also say, I wouldn't turn down a text, email, snap, or DM either — especially from my kids and grandkids who are digital natives! This grandma understands that digital is their world.

I hope that you can find some concrete and practical ideas here that will help you to transform your life from wherever you are now, to begin creating and living your ideal life, day by day and moment by moment, knowing you have a future and a hope backed with a gratitude mindset.

MEET STEFANY DOLAN

Stefany is a wife, mother, and executive with *becauseOne*. After over 11 years as a dental hygienist, she made the jump alongside the rest of her family to create and launch *becauseOne*. She feels at home in the stillness of the country, but is always willing to drive to visit family, friends or enjoy a good meal. She enjoys being barefoot in her garden, appreciates time in her kitchen canning and baking, and relishes a good 2:00 coffee.

Website: https://becauseone.com/

Facebook: https://www.facebook.com/profile.php?id=100087037890605

Instagram: https://www.instagram.com/becauseone_community/

LinkedIn: https://www.linkedin.com/company/becauseone

Personal LinkedIn Page: https://www.linkedin.com/in/stefany-dolan-925968b0/

Email: info@becauseOne.com

Phone number: 463-444-8301

A DOUBTFUL VOICE TURNED CONFIDENT

By: Stefany Dolan

If someone were to ask me who I am or what I do, I would say that I'm a wife, a mother, and a woman who owns and helps run a business called *becauseOne*. It's a business that helps some of the most interesting and important nonprofits you can imagine. On top of that, it's a business that brings me joy, fulfillment, and flexibility I was not sure would ever be attainable.

I can see how this simple explanation sounds like a dream. If I'm being honest, it is!! There's a story behind how I got here. There have been a lot of ups, downs, and teaching moments that have made me the businesswoman I am today.

I think it is most appropriate that we start from the beginning.

I graduated with a degree in dental hygiene at the ripe age of twenty-two. Soon after graduation, I landed a full-time position in a great dental office. I quickly became the lead hygienist and was helping run the hygiene department. I had a four-day work week, was sent out of state for business training, and made good connections with patients and other employees. What more could a new grad want?!

After settling in and gaining my footing for a year or two, my mind started to wonder during my long commute to and from work. "What if we tried a new strategy in the hygiene department?" or "What if I implemented *this* process in the office?" I was constantly thinking of new ways to grow. After a while, I felt like I was hitting the ceiling of the hygiene department. I had this feeling that I would never be able to break through.

My uncle, Dr. Greg Winteregg, a successful dentist and well known in the dental consulting world, reached out with an idea. He knew of a *very* successful out-of-state dental practice he thought my family and I should visit. We went for a quick visit and toured two or three of their ten established dental offices. I saw multiple dental offices humming. People who needed dental care were having their needs met. Employees were hardworking. Upper management's focus was on growing the business by investing in employees. I. Was. Hooked. But where did I fit into this business model? The answer to that question left me literally speechless.

I could be their first dental office out of state. The plan was, I would be trained in their largest dental office to gain experience and see a wide range of scenarios. I would also have the opportunity to travel out of state to personal development and business growth seminars. Then, after six months, I would have the training and knowledge necessary to open a brand-new dental office! Their first office out of state. I would have great success if I simply did what the other successful offices did. This is a no brainer, right?

Then a doubtful voice in my head chimed in, "Can you do this? You're just a 20-something dental hygienist! How could anyone trust *you* to run a business AND start it from scratch in a brand-new market?".

After much thought, many prayers, and long talks with family, friends, and my trusted uncle, I jumped headfirst into the unknown. I squashed that doubtful voice and replaced it with one of confidence. "There's no way this won't work! I'm a smart, capable woman, surrounded by a great team. We've GOT THIS!"

Excitedly — with a little nervousness cooked in — I moved out of state into a furnished apartment and started learning and growing. Oh my, was it fun! I was working some long hours, but we were helping a lot of people. There were plenty of difficult situations to navigate with employees, upper management, and patients, but I was learning something new every day. My favorite part was the employees I worked with. They became my out of state family. It was difficult being away from family and friends, missing big events (like my best friend's wedding festivities, and other big life moments), but I held onto the fact that I would be back home in six months.

Then six months came and went. There was no sign of my dream office being completed or me going home. That doubtful voice chimed back in, "Maybe this is a sign. Why don't you just head home and let them get the office ironed out. *Then* you can get the ball rolling again". After discussions with close family and friends, I kept the faith and was willing to stay longer. I chose to look at this as an opportunity to be more prepared for opening day. Plus, I got to stay longer with some fun, wonderful people. I learned more about HR, traveled to more seminars, and had the opportunity to work at many of their successful offices. I was able to take little tokens of knowledge from each one.

A thread that was woven through all the practices was that the office manager needed a right-hand person. This person would help run the back office while the office manager oversaw the front and helped manage the back. That doubtful voice in my head came back. "You don't know how to hire people! How will you even begin to train someone and have them ready? Where in the world will you find this person?" Then it came to me. The person closest to me in the world. My sister.

My sister was finishing her criminal justice degree and was graduating in a couple of weeks. I called her just before she was finalizing her post-graduation plans. With just the right amount of hesitation, she agreed. It only made sense that she would be my right-hand person; she always had been! We worked out a schedule for her to train with me. In a few weeks, she moved in, and we hit the ground running!

Finally, my dream office was underway. As the office was getting closer to being finished, my sister and I were traveling home more. We worked closely with the contractor to get the office to the finish line. After the final inspection, we were ready to accept patients. The excitement was palpable! How would this *not* work?! We had several successful offices to model after and supportive management. What could go wrong?

This is how it was supposed to go. My sister and I would train and open the doors. Patients would flood into our new, beautiful practice. We would work long, strenuous hours, help a lot of people, and set record highs within a couple of months!

This is the reality of how it went. Sometimes our phones would go all day without ringing (expect for the random spam phone call). At times, patients who needed treatment could not (or would not) get their treatment completed. Things just were not taking off as quickly as they had with other offices. Business was *slowww*.

During this time, we were in close contact with our out-of-state owners and upper management. We were always trying to work on the problem and battle plan. At the beginning, this was a fun puzzle that certainly had a perfect solution. As we got deeper, a small crack became a gaping chasm. The people I worked with for several years were and are wonderful people. Their dental offices are businesses to be reckoned with. I was forced to take a stance for myself and decide what I was and was not willing to do for my career. This is where the chasm started.

My brain was always working. From the second I woke up I was thinking of what I could implement to make this business work. It was during these critical thinking times, I started to notice some stark differences between how the out-of-state offices were run and how my office was run. I started sharing my new perspectives with management. At times, I was proposing some drastic changes to the previously successful model. My sister and I were on phone call after phone call sharing our observations and possible solutions. Over time, two sisters who stood tall in confidence were slowly chipped away. Over time, we grew smaller and smaller.

We suggested limiting weekend hours because Saturdays were slow. Patients would much rather use PTO to take a Tuesday morning off so they could go to their kid's soccer game on Saturday morning.

Management: There needs to be willingness on your part to be at the office to help people!

Chip.

Our office sat right on the edge of two different zip codes. I suggested we increase marketing north of our office based on the demographics I had researched.

Management: What we really need is more boots on the ground! Can you come in on your day off to market to local businesses and apartment buildings?

Chip.

We suggested changes when scheduling patients so we had more control of our schedule and patients would not have to wait for their appointments. At times we were running more than an hour behind.

Management: When a patient is there, you help them! They'll be willing to wait. People behind their appointment will understand.

Chip.

I suggested changes in our work schedules to help reprieve burnout. We needed time to be with friends, family, and to unwind after working 12+ hour days.

Management: When starting a new business, you must be willing to push through! We need to see your willingness to make this work.

Chip.

We said, "yes" to whatever the ask was. The doubtful voice grew louder. "You don't know what you're doing. You're just an over trained hygienist. Just listen to what they ask and eventually this will turn around."

Chip.

Chip.

I kept quiet. My sister and I did it all. We became flakey friends who cancelled dinner plans at the last minute. At one point, we worked thirteen days to have one Sunday off. Once we had an agreement to have Wednesdays off, these "days off" became a day to catch up at the office. We took early calls on the commute to work and in the car on the way home. I started to share less of my ideas and started to feel guilt for putting my sister in a situation that seemed to have no light at the end of the tunnel.

At work, I did my best to put my "sister" title aside and put my businesswoman hat on. I listened as she battled with upper management for a fair wage. I struggled as I asked her to stay late and cancel plans in the name of willingness. Eventually, my sister just couldn't take it anymore.

One day she called me. She cried (a lot) and told me she needed to be in a place where she felt valued and could have some work/life balance. I watched her go from being so hungry for growth to being a person who was so far from herself. She graciously gave me six weeks to find a replacement. I think deep down I knew this was the start of the fall.

I never found a replacement. I was working double duty. The office seemed to be failing. Then I got a phone call.

I got fired. Then they asked to hire me back, but that's another story. At the time I was about as low as I could get.

"You knew you couldn't do this! See, you *are* the problem. Maybe you subconsciously *were* unwilling to make this work. Man, what a failure!"

I was a smaller version of my former self and full to the brim with doubt. What was once a confident, capable 20 something hygienist became a deflated, constantly second guessing, failed businesswoman.

When reflecting on the next phase of my dental career and life, it can be broken down into three stages: Sadness & Heartbreak, Gratitude and "What's Next". Each of these stages brought growth, reflection, and plenty of teaching moments.

Sadness & Heartbreak
This is when that doubtful voice was the loudest. During this stage, I let myself be sad, feel big feelings, and battled with shame and embarrassment. After some time to heal, I had to acknowledge that I've sat, run countless scenarios through my head during too many sleepless nights, and now it was time to get up and find a safe place to move on.

I had my hygiene license. I knew I could help offices as a substitute hygienist. On this new journey, I chose to set healthy work/home boundaries. I made my own schedule, worked hard, but also made time for my family and friends. For a few months, I worked at many offices filling in when their hygienists were out. It was a wonderful learning experience and helped me see what I would want in a more permanent position.

Gratitude
At this point, I had been helping numerous offices for 3–4 months. I was finding happiness in my career again. The pain and chaos of the roller coaster ride had subsided. I could feel grateful for the journey. I had experience in some of the most productive dental offices in the field. I had the opportunity to meet some wonderful people who were doing great things. I could separate the downfall into a box of "something that happened." I used it as a gauge of where I was not willing to go again in my career. I was no longer willing to give up big life events or be a flaky friend.

One day, I was subbing at Hardin Cosmetic & Family Dentistry. It was the best office! At lunch, I called my husband and told him that if they ever had a full-time position open, I would HAPPILY drive an hour to work there! With a little luck and timing, a few weeks later, Dr. Hardin called me with a full-time position. I found my people. I found my voice, and the doubtful voice grew quieter.

This dental office was more than a job, it became a family. We grew as a team, shared ideas and perspectives with each other. I used the knowledge I gained during my experience in running an office to share some different perspectives with the dentist and the team. I grew with this team through the start of my marriage, the birth of my two children, and all the highs and lows in between. My confidence started to grow. I was at peace.

"What's next?"
Alongside my newfound sense of peace, I found myself wondering how I could make a difference, dreaming bigger. Sure, having set hours, a three-day weekend every week, feeling valued in my workplace, and working with an excellent dentist and fellow employees was a blessing!
There was this inkling that I could do more; that I was meant for more.

Then, my sister called me again.

She started working with our dad's financial advising firm after she left the dental office. They had been working together on an idea outside of the financial world. A *really* big idea! This was the kind of idea that could change our lives, the lives of others within our communities, and across the country. I was in! This was the nudge I needed.

After two or three years of diligent planning, lots of prayer, and leaps of faith, as a family, we created a business called *becauseOne*. My sister and I were back as a dynamic duo. We're helping nonprofits have more sustainability, support their communities, bringing awareness to important causes, and sharing the joy as humans help other humans!

Without my teardown and rebuild, I am certain that I would not have the same skills I have today. I've taken these teaching moments and evolved them. Yes, boundaries are of course important! That being said, it is also important to analyze, take a step back and be flexible.

When there's an ask within my work life, I take a step back and see if it aligns with my goals and the nonprofits I'm supporting. If it makes sense, the answer is, "yes,". It's okay if it lands on a Friday night.

Having my voice back comes with the deep need to listen. Helping run a start-up includes many important players. My ears must be open to new ideas. My mind must be open to pivots in processes and strategies. My voice is not just there to be loud and heard, it is there to bring value and help move the business forward.

Through it all, I've dreamed big. Early on, I wanted more than working a hygiene schedule. I jumped into management with a large dental corporation. The roller coaster of that journey could have squelched my desire to make that vulnerable leap again. That burn for more persisted. Through these experiences and teaching moments, I have gained my confidence back.

I am a capable, 30-something businesswoman who is here with my eyes on the sky.

As a family, we took a leap of faith. Being the owner of a startup company has its ups and downs. I look at the nonprofit organizations we are helping, and I *know* we are making a difference.

That doubtful voice still tries to sneak its way in at times. Now, I take a quick listen and tell it to move aside. My sister and I take pride in our growth. We have proved that we *are* willing to work late. We *are* willing to bend over backward to help. We *are* a strong, capable women who can solve just about any problem that comes our way.

Lookout world, my sister and I are a force to be reckoned with. The future is bright!

MEET STACIA JONES

Stacia is a woman of many hats: wife, licensed financial advisor assistant, and executive with *becauseOne*. While helping run the family financial advising firm, she took lead with the development and launch of *becauseOne*. She enjoys a fun day out with her husband equally as much as a day at home relaxing, watching movies or reading a book. Stacia earned a Bachelor of Science in Criminal Justice so it's no surprise she often still dabbles in crime documentaries and podcasts. She loves her Jeep almost as much as her dog. Her humor is witty and she's always good for a one liner.

You can contact Stacia here:

Website: https://becauseone.com/
Facebook: https://www.facebook.com/profile.php?id=100087037890605
Instagram: https://www.instagram.com/becauseone_community
LinkedIn: becauseOne

- https://www.linkedin.com/company/becauseone

Stacia Jones

- https://www.linkedin.com/in/staciawinteregg

Phone number: 463-444-8301

FROM IDEA TO IMPACT: HOW ONE FAMILY'S IDEA IS TRANSFORMING LIVES

By: Stacia Jones

Remember the sister from Stefany's story? Well, that's me, Stacia!

Although my experience was similar to my sister's, my exit provided the space for a thought to spawn into an idea. That idea blossomed into reality. The idea: a company whose purpose is to transform lives for the better. Along the way, it happened to transform my life and my heart, too!

Prior to my last day at the dental office, I started my job search. Holding a bachelor's degree in criminal justice, I sought to dive into my field of interest. Life, God, and my dad had other plans. As I was finalizing my resume, my dad was searching for a much-needed team member.

Since 1985, my dad, Jon, has been an independent financial advisor. After shadowing him for my senior year internship in high school, I was certain the financial industry was not for me. Things change. Once my dad knew I was going to be floating my resume and booking interviews, he humbly asked, "Can I throw my name in the hat?".

My initial reaction was to decline. Before I could say no, my dad requested a simple meeting. He tasked me with outlining what I would like my future and new career path to look like in the next one year, five years, and ten years.

We sat down at Buffalo Wild Wings in February 2016. I had my notes compiled and ready. I envisioned the meeting would end by me breaking the news to my dad gently; I would be going in another direction. The respect for my dad, his excitement about the possibility of hiring me, and a small seed of curiosity kept me in the booth. I was open to learning and seeking to be a part of a professional team where individuals' strengths were celebrated, utilized, and trusted. Looking back, I realize the wisdom he had to focus the conversation on the environment he could provide and what my role may entail, versus discussing the opportunities the industry could offer.

My list of goals and expectations went a little something like this:

Year One–Get comfortable. Grasp a meaningful level of understanding. Regain confidence and work life balance.
Year Five–Attain a leadership position where I can utilize my love for people, visionary mindset, and creativity.
Year Ten–Freedom to continue to grow. Be able to clearly see how my role and God-given talents are truly making a difference.

After laying out all my expectations, desired responsibilities, and vision, my dad flipped over his list. What he was seeking in a new team member and the environment he wished to provide was in great alignment with what I was searching for.

"When can I start?"

The meeting with my dad and our discussion taught me the power of keeping an open mind. Many times, we fail to fully view a decision from multiple angles, because we think we already know what the path might look like. Don't fall victim to this fortune-telling trap!

Informing my sister I needed to move on was heartbreaking. I loved working with my sister. The last thing I wanted to do was leave her stranded on the hamster wheel. After all, we still managed to have fun during our time working together! However, like the amazing, supportive sister she is, she was happy for me. Little did I know at the time, our professional paths would cross again a few years later.

I was excited for the next chapter, welcoming it as a time to heal, regain my confidence, and to find Stacia again. I wanted to be me again — the tireless visionary whose creativity, wit, intelligence, and big picture outlook on life brings people together, provides clarity, and even adds a bit of fun to the toughest of situations.

My Dad believed in me and empowered me when I was second guessing my own strengths. Using my prior training, and through my dad's guidance, I created processes, workflows, and procedures that equipped our team to better serve our clients. I was enjoying creating new aspects to the client service experience — I was regaining confidence and finding myself again!

Once the workflows and processes were refined and running smoothly, like any entrepreneur, I got bored. When you're bored, look for the next challenge. Mine was to earn all the necessary licenses to become a financial advisor. Hands down, this was the hardest I had ever studied in my life. In February 2017, I passed my Series 7 on my very first attempt!

After passing my all my tests, I began serving our clients in a whole new way. I looked forward to learning current plans and implementing new ones as a team with my dad. I loved being a part of guiding clients from a place of uncertainty to a path of confidence and clarity. People looked as if a weight had physically been removed from their shoulders when they left our office. Dad and I were the dream team!

One of the most fulfilling strategies we implemented was for nonprofit organizations. The strategy allowed nonprofits to place safety nets into their financial plans that furthered their ability to carry out and focus on their missions. Soon, we were helping multiple local nonprofit organizations. Although our team was doing good work and making a difference for these organizations, something was missing.

Then we remembered what happened in 2005.

When I was growing up, my family and I were members of a church that was growing rapidly. The church held a large capital campaign to raise funds for a much-needed children and youth wing. People were generous. The money was raised; the building was built, but there were not enough funds to furnish the space.

Luckily, my dad had an idea. What if people knew what the church needed to finish the new wing? Maybe this could re-inspire a congregation who already went "all in". A catalog was created that clearly listed the wide variety of necessary items needed: trees, tables and chairs, playground equipment, drinking fountains, fire extinguishers, and even the ability to sponsor a classroom in your name. There was truly a way for everyone to make a difference, and the book communicated that!

The book was distributed, but how would the congregation respond? Immediately, inspiration and excitement flooded through the pews. After defining what was needed, people responded in a big way. Those who had already been generous, gave again. Many who hadn't given or felt as though what they could contribute wasn't enough, quickly acted as soon as they felt connected to a specific item within their means. Months later, the building was furnished and used to guide children and youth to Christ.

As a daughter and little girl, it was a meaningful experience to see my dad updating the congregation every Sunday, "The trees have been given! Now we need chalkboards, area rugs, and cribs. And don't forget there are naming opportunities that allow you to sponsor the nursery, a classroom, or the upstairs wing". I even took some of my allowance to purchase a need — suddenly I, as a little girl, was understanding the value of giving.

Now to 2019. I can vividly recall my dad nearly running down the hall to my office, "Stacia, these nonprofits need a catalog! How do we get them a catalog?"

Immediately, my brain went to work. An idea was growing. We couldn't print books for all the nonprofits we currently served, let alone others we wanted to help. We needed an online platform — a virtual catalog. Being a millennial, I knew the power of technology and social media firsthand. We could create a virtual book, but more than that, we could create a platform that could further the reach of an organization's mission and inspire others along the way!

Notes on iPhones, weekly meetings at Coffeehouse Five, late-night phone calls — the idea, the dream was growing. What if there was a place online where anyone could go to make a difference? What if nonprofits could clearly and consistently communicate what they need? What if someone, a total stranger, could be directly connected to the needs of others based on their own interests? The sports lover providing basketball shoes to a kid; the construction worker providing tools; the retired teacher providing art supplies to a classroom; the '90s kid providing Chutes & Ladders and Candyland to a girl's program, and the doctor providing care or a prosthetic to a veteran. What would it mean if there was one place online where people could go to see good happening? How could we take one positive action and position it to inspire the next good deed?

becauseOne.com was formed. Now our family really got to work. The idea, the notes, and the outlines were too loud to ignore any longer. God was pulling our family down a new path.

As God's perfect timing may have it, a close family friend of ours was in the beginning stages of developing a platform for attorneys, built by attorneys, *Inheralink*. He got us in touch with *Reusser* out of Roanoke, Indiana. After a discovery call and signed nondisclosure agreements, the *Reusser* team came to the Southside to learn more.

In preparation, Dad and I created an outline of all the features the platform would need. Up to this point, no one outside of the family had heard the idea. Were we just dreaming? Would the experts tell us all our thought, collaboration, and work up to this point was done in vain? We pushed through the fear and doubt — we had to know *how* becauseOne.com could be created.

Our presentation clearly outlined four main pillars of *becauseOne.com*:

1. Item Based Giving – Nonprofit Organizations and their teams are the groups and individuals that truly know the needs of our communities and our nation. *becauseOne* provides a place where each nonprofit organization has a dedicated online page where they can clearly communicate, define, and essentially register for their needs. Take the "how are you going to spend the money" question off the table. When nonprofits take the time to really communicate what they need, it helps everyone see how

they can help. Not to mention, when people can clearly visualize the impact their donation dollars are having, they experience more joy as they are helping others. We miss the mark and rob each other of the true happiness of helping one another when we fail to communicate exactly how donation dollars are transforming lives.

2. Further Reach Through Automatic Connection – Many people want to help others, but don't know where to start or what the needs exists. Our technology allows every person, business, foundation, or corporation to start with what they know best — their passions. From there, our technology automatically connects them to needs and nonprofits within their area of interest! This technology brings people together across state lines and works to help further the reach of the nonprofits.

3. Social Engagement – Giving is a highly transactional experience. Outside of traditional fundraising events, there is little room allowing for one good deed to truly inspire the next. On becauseOne.com people can follow nonprofits, family, and friends to stay up to date on good happening all around them. Now, instead of sitting down and writing checks or giving to an organization through other online platforms, that same good deed has the energy to inspire the next! On *becauseOne* any time a good deed occurs, that positive action starts a ripple effect throughout the network of followers. Now a chain reaction of good deeds can begin!

4. Sponsorship – Many families and businesses wanted to "put their name on a room" during the church catalog days. We wanted to give these same groups the ability to sponsor their favorite organization on *becauseOne*. This sponsorship allows a generous donor to provide a nonprofit of their choosing with the technology and expert *becauseOne* team at no cost to the nonprofit. Families and

businesses can personalize their sponsorship in memory of a loved one, in recognition of key employees, or in celebration of a milestone moment. But rather than this sponsorship being a one-time gift, the family members and friends, teams and coworkers can follow along as differences are being made throughout the entirety of the year!

After our presentation, the experts looked around the room at one another. Not only did they love the idea, but they also had the team to build *becauseOne.com*! God put the right people in the room. Our teams immediately had great synergy and collaboration.

However, due diligence must be completed. *Reusser* needed to do a deep dive. This discovery process would outline what features would be needed and total costs. There was one semi-skeptical team member, Brandon, who would be tasked with figuring out if someone had already created the idea.

"I like the idea, but I'm in charge of going back to my desk and blowing it up. I need to prove it's already been done, and that your money and time would be better spent elsewhere." He was so confident he would be able to prove why our team should close shop before we had even begun. "This just makes too much sense to not have already been created."

We anxiously awaited the results of discovery and Brandon's findings.

A few weeks later, the *Reusser* team led us through a proposal. Although we were excited to know becauseOne.com could be built, it was overwhelming. Not only were the costs huge, but the technological language was foreign to us.
They opened with Brandon's findings. He searched far and wide. Although he found a handful of online platforms doing parts of what

we wanted to accomplish, no one was marrying up all four pillars in the meaningful way we were seeking. No platform had all the magic of *becauseOne*!

Once the discussion shifted from walking us through features and numbers, a couple *Reusser* team members shared their stories and personal thoughts.

Brandon shared his childhood experience as a baseball player. He not only loved playing baseball but had a deep love for the game. Year after year, due to lack of family resources, he would play with the same beat-up baseball glove. He recalled the embarrassment of starting each season with a worn-out mitt alongside his teammate's fresh, new mitts.

Emotionally, Brandon instructed, "You must do this. You have to build *becauseOne*, because I need the opportunity to buy a kid in need a baseball glove."

On May 16, 2023, Brandon donated a baseball glove to a kid in need on becauseOne.com. A profound, full circle moment.

Austin, a lead developer, shared, "If you need to investigate other development companies, I understand. However, even if you don't hire our team, you need to move forward with making this idea a reality. This experience must exist. The world needs it."

I have held on to Austin's words and Brandon's story many times as we navigated bringing becauseOne.com to launch day.

We attempted raising capital for about a year to help us tackle the burden of cost. Although we landed meetings with many investors who were "leaning in the whole time", the doors were not opening.

Back to the drawing board. This time we used our phone-a-friend lifeline. This "friend" happened to be my uncle, Dr. Greg Winteregg. We watched as his wheels started spinning. Uncle Greg posed a different perspective we hadn't explored yet. Greg encouraged us to determine how we, as a family, could get the process started without any investors. Was there a way we could dial back the original proposal to a more manageable cost while still building all four necessary pillars? Staying open minded and exploring outside perspectives served us well once more.

A new proposal was drafted that still accomplished the experience envisioned. Although our team remained open-minded to other ways forward, we never sacrificed any of the four *becauseOne* pillars. We would be able to fund and tackle the development of *becauseOne* as a family.

Before we could share with Uncle Greg that his guidance helped us with this critical decision, he passed away unexpectedly. We miss his knowledge, never tiring energy, and desire to help others daily. Throughout this journey, our family makes a conscious effort to not miss a moment to acknowledge where Uncle Greg would be proud, celebrating our wins, or laughing right alongside us as we experience the many aspects of owning and running a business.

Development started. I was the main point of communication as *Reusser* built becauseOne.com. We had weekly meetings going over, defining, and refining different features and experiences. I had to learn how to ask the right questions, communicate our vision, and lead our team and *Reusser* through the process.

Of all my accomplishments, leading our team and building our partnership with *Reusser* will make its way to the top of my list forever. I learned how to speak a different language and coach my team through significant decisions. I had to understand how one tweak could alter an experience, sometimes for the better and other times with many unintended consequences. I had to learn when to dig my heals in and not compromise our original vision, and when to dive deeper into a solution I had never thought of.

Communication and synergy are key with any team and any partnership. Not only must you keep your vision and mission at the forefront, but you must know how to clearly communicate those goals to others. The trust and respect between our team and *Reusser* is deeply profound. Our goals are in perfect alignment, allowing us to pull in the same direction while bringing our individual strengths to the table to achieve the best possible result!

One of my most used phrases with our lead developer, Jake, went like this, "Okay, Jake. I'm going to tell you how I think this feature should work. Then, I need you to tell me where I'm wrong or where we can make it better!". More times than not, Jake would be able to elevate the vision, educate me on why that would create a clunky experience, or ask questions to further understand our desire. This highly collaborative partnership yielded the best possible experience during development. There were a few times Jake would respond with, "I like it! That makes sense. I'll get to work!". Those times built my confidence and helped my inner voice say, "Hey I am starting to get the hang of this whole development thing!".

About 2 months away from launching becauseOne.com, as marketing plans and final testing were being completed, a monumental hurdle presented itself. During development, I was still juggling my full-time role at the financial firm. In the financial industry, even in independent firms, offices rely on the efficiency of their "back-office", or broker dealer, to process their client requests in a timely manner. Regardless of our diligent follow-up and attention to detail, our team's and our clients' requests were not being handled in an effective manner. We were going to need to change back offices. This would include repapering about 1,000 accounts. All new paperwork, all new signatures from every single client.

I had this monumental challenge at the financial firm transpiring in tandem with the *becauseOne* launch timeline. The back-office change would not have been even remotely possible without our outstanding Client Service Manager, Kurtis, who led our team and clients through the change in about six weeks. This is unheard of. We came together to get the job done. Kurtis' leadership and never-ending willingness was inspirational, admirable, and quite impressive. I may be a little bias, as I am also proud to call Kurtis my husband but ask anyone—it was amazing! We even spent our second-year anniversary at the office until about 4:00 a.m. cranking out paperwork for our clients. What a memory!

During this challenge at the financial firm, I was unable to focus on the final efforts needed to get *becauseOne.com* launched. We needed someone to keep things moving. My sister came back into the picture. Although she helped with vision, testing, and decisions outside of her current dental hygiene role, she was not a full time *becauseOne* team member. God made it clear to all of us that now was the time to reunite sisters in business.

After the back-office change and launch of *becauseOne,* our family felt a genuine sense of freedom. We were finally able to be with a team who handled our clients' requests with care and *becauseOne.com* was officially launched on October 25, 2022!

I am blessed to work alongside my family. The missions of each company center around serving others. *becauseOne* seeks to transform lives: Transform the life of someone in need, transform the heart of those willing and able to help, and transform the way nonprofits communicate. In turn, it has also transformed the life of my family as we have experienced our dream come to life together. Working with my sister is a true gift. Our strengths are different, our perspectives are different, and that is exactly what makes us unstoppable. I would not want to celebrate wins or navigate tough decisions with anyone else by my side.

I am humbled to be a part of *becauseOne*. It's something that has quickly become so much bigger than me. I have been able to sit back and watch as lives are being transformed. Nonprofits now have access to the tools and team the industry has been missing. In just a year, I am witnessing a community coming together, good deeds inspiring the next, and happiness spreading. *becauseOne* is truly proving that because one person helps another, because one positive action can lead to the next, our world and our hearts will never be the same.

For anyone with an idea, nurture it. Pay attention to the open doors and where God is leading you. Stay open minded. Align yourself with others smarter than you and with expertise in areas foreign to you. Always communicate your vision clearly, learn how to pivot communication when needed, have fun along the way, and keep serving others as your top priority. When you seek to help others, you will create something bigger than yourself, then hang on and enjoy the ride.

MEET ANGIE WOOD

Angela (Angie) Larrabee-Wood lives in Carmel, Indiana. I am a mother of three children. My passion and reason for writing is to love and encourage people to live the life God has for them. Life is a precious gift you never want to take for granted. I was a severe trauma victim who many questioned would live and recover. However, in this story you will see God still performs miracles and saved my life.

My hobbies are reading, writing, encouraging people, building strong Community relationships. I love the youth and inspiring them. Total Wellness, sports, yoga and exercise have been my lifelong passions. The Lord is my anchor and everything. I hope you find hope and encouragement as you read my story. Love to you all.

Angela Larrabee-Wood

AGAINST ALL ODDS, BUT GOD!

By: Angie Wood

Have you ever encountered a trial, grief, or hardship that completely shipwrecked your life or changed it drastically? Have you ever experienced how a journey of true growth and hope inspired you to greatness? Well, let me share my journey and inspire, encourage you in true freedom, growth, and purpose, an anchor that has not moved in the storms of life.

Eight years ago, I experienced severe trauma in ways I never imagined could happen to anyone. The trauma froze me to a state of complete body lock up and cognitive difficulties. I got to a point where I could hardly move, speak, or process. Anxiety completely took over me to a crippling degree. I had never experienced anything like this I my entire life. I never knew trauma could be this severe. I lost all hope and love for life. I was completely frozen. Moving forward the best I could after hospitalization, which caused more trauma, I now realized I could not be independent. I had to be under care with a medical treatment team to work on getting my life back. During my journey of recovery, I had to come to grips emotionally and physically with the fact that I had a long hard road ahead of me.

Eight years ago, I was struck with a metal vase in the back of my head. I went into shock instantly. I did not realize until exploring my physical condition that I had suffered a traumatic brain injury, PTSD, and severe trauma. That diagnosis was very hard for me to face because I thought my career and life were gone. Getting my life back and accepting the new normal was going to be long, painful, and hard. I had to let go of my dreams and the destiny I had and begin to accept the new normal the Lord had for me.

The first verse the Lord gave me over and over before the trial hit was Jeremiah 29:11. Paraphrased, it states that, *"For I know the plans I have for you, plans to prosper you and not to harm you, plans to give you hope and a future."* That was my anchor from God to get through this trial. I wish I could say the journey was short lived. It was the longest, hardest journey I had ever endured. We were not sure I was going to make it.

Due to the severity of my trauma, I lost everything: My home, career, belongings, health, cognitive and verbal abilities; my parents and two friends passed away, and I lost my family to some degree. Everything was gone in a moment. I was overwhelmed without hope to say the least. This left me in a state of panic, grief, despair, and hopelessness. I had never encountered grief to a state of almost death like that. I was losing weight daily, unable to process, and dying internally from all the pain and loss. My kids, dreams, career, and life I felt was gone instantly. To be honest and transparent, I wanted to die. I had lost all hope. Every time I tried to talk and reach out to my kids, my body would lock up and I could not speak. I would just cry and cry. I had no other choice but to seek out medical treatment to help me get my life back.

The first support I received was from a skills specialist, Carla Jones. She was a Godsend. It took her three years just to get me to talk and share what had happened to me. I needed to do some deep healing and come out of my fear and isolation. This new normal was very hard to accept. I was no longer the outgoing, talkative, passionate, hardworking, and encouraging strong community leader I had been before. I was now faced with the new normal of dealing with severe anxiety, PTSD, panic attacks, grief, and a traumatic brain injury.

To look at the whole journey at once, it seemed like a very hopeless journey. The whole process of recovering was trauma in itself. The hardest thing I experienced was realizing that our society needs to be educated in the areas of trauma and PTSD. I went through a lot of pain due to ignorance. I began to understand the many obstacles in recovering from trauma, grief, anxiety, traumatic brain injury, and PTSD. A difficult part of the healing process was from the outside; after a few years, I looked capable. However, the exterior appearance belied everything I had endured in those years.

The Lord began to heal and inspire me one step at a time. He inspired me to create a piece of artwork that hangs in the lobby of my doctor's offices. He gave me the title," A Miracle of New Beginnings." The Lord gave me a vision of what he wanted me to paint. He had me paint sketch marks of grey on the outer part with a big heart in the center. The heart had a black border which He later showed me represented my trauma. On the inside of the heart were beautiful bright colors, which represented that my heart would be full of color, light, joy, and full of hope again. He laid on my heart to write the word GRACE on the outside of the heart.

First, this was amazing to me because I'm not good at art. It encouraged me so much. It wasn't until a year later that He started doing the work on my heart and bringing about in my life what He created through me on my canvas. The Holy Spirit began to change my heart and mind. The Lord began to heal me and give me a whole new perspective and clarity. Scriptures began to flood into my life, seeing the word of God in a whole new revelation. Romans 8:28, Jeremiah 29:11, the story of Joseph, Job, the book of Proverbs. The list goes on. I spent eight years doing treatment, deep therapy, healing,

Bible studies, worship, and most importantly, just sitting and listening to God. It was a miraculous work of new perspectives, teaching, healing, and clarity by the Holy Spirit.

Little did I know the Lord was showing me and teaching me His work of GRACE and LOVE in amazing ways. A new beginning had sprung! Through much work with a therapist, skills specialist, Bible studies, worship, and steps of faith by me, my life was starting to turn around. The mental part was healed, and I continued to work on the PTSD and triggering parts. I went through brain injury rehab and cognitive therapy. The work it took from me, and my treatment team was very long and difficult, but well worth all the effort. I listened and took very difficult steps; I processed my grief and trauma through therapy. I was deeply honest, transparent, and authentic, which helped me to heal deeply within.

Every step I took, God blessed me so much. The only way I could heal, and recover was to make myself do the impossible steps that gave me healing. I had to face my trauma, brain injury, and PTSD barriers, and deal with things one step at a time. It was a frustrating process because it took a lot of patience and went very slowly. Words cannot express all the wisdom, revelations, perspective changes, and clarity I received from the Lord throughout this journey I was on. A big take away is: The Lord gives us passion, puts things in our hearts, equips us to fulfill His purpose in our lives and community.

Psalms 139 shows us He is the one who knitted us in our mother's womb, created us with gifts, talents, and purpose. What are you doing with your gifts and talents? Are you a good steward with them, making a difference in other people's lives and in your community? He wants to use all of us to create positive change and teach community leadership and values along the way. Don't ever hesitate to be brave and courageous, to step out and do what you love. The Lord puts those desires and passions in us.

God has taken certain things in my life and brought purpose, hope, change, and growth to me and the community. He took tragedy and totally transformed my life in a wonderful way (Romans 8:28). The Lord has enabled me now to do those things I'm gifted to do without stress. True contentment, freedom, and joy rule my life now (Jeremiah 29:11, Psalms 91).

I think one of the saddest things I've seen in society is that people do not give self-love to themselves. We cannot truly love others if we don't purely love ourselves. Mindfulness, self-care, and being transparent, teachable, humble, and deeply authentic are some of the best ways we can heal. God is the healer, and He teaches us many things in deep trials, trauma, and grief. The disappointing thing is that many get angry at God in hard times and run from Him, shut Him out. Without the work of the Holy Spirit to teach, heal, and give insight, we can't recover and heal deeply within. When we totally surrender all of it to the Lord, He does miraculous things, heals, and gives much wisdom on living life through Him.

One of the best things God did for me on my recovery journey was teach me to lean into Him strongly and be a good listener. Do what He speaks in your heart to do. He removed the people, obstacles, and anything that was conflicting with His perfect will for my life. I had to open to Him deeply to allow Him to heal me and help me do what He has called me to do. I began to truly know who I am in Christ and who I belong to. I went through five years of trauma recover, PTSD training, therapy, and brain rehabilitation. All these things together and the Lord brought me so much wisdom and healing.

I surrendered every day to Him and allowed Him to completely take over. It was the best thing I could have every done for myself. I dug deep, reflected, and let the Lord do the work that only He can do. He did the impossible for me. I give Him all the glory. I gained so much Godly wisdom, clarity, revelations, and insights. Taking time out and committing to do the inner deep work with the Lord and His Spirit is so rewarding and an example of self-love. The gratitude that has been placed in my heart that I can now live life fully with true freedom, joy, and happiness is a miracle. I'm so thankful to be alive and that God gave me breath and another day. That which was at one time totally impossible, the Lord made possible. I knew at that point I was going to make it and knew I could trust God in all things no matter how impossible they seemed.

In today's world, with so much controversy, trauma, negativity, and narcissism, it's a great feeling to pause, read the word, listen to the Lord, worship, do therapy, and do the work it takes to have mental health, wholeness, and total wellness. The scripture states, *"Do not conform to the ways of the world but be transformed by the renewing of your mind."* To walk in God's Wisdom and ways. That's where true inner peace and joy are found. My anchor and hope are in the one who truly created me, gifted me, and has given me new hope and purpose. We are destined to bring positive change and true authentic leadership to this world.

Many people in our world are struggling with anxiety and mental health issues, and they have lost their self-awareness and inner peace. I'm truly grateful for all the knowledge, depth, Godly wisdom, and new perspectives on life He has given me. He has called me to serve and help bring new growth and values back to society. To mentor and help our youth. In life we have all gone through different types of traumas, hardships, or grief; some small, others severe. However, through everything we encounter, we have an opportunity to reflect, gain wisdom, and grow deeper. I have now gained a new life, new freedom, growth, expansion, wisdom, broader perspectives, grace, and love from the Father in ways I never dreamed possible. I have truly learned from experience what Romans 8:28 really means: The Lord's promise to us that He brings all things together for the good of those who truly love and serve Him. He has brought to my life so many promises that are in His Word.

I challenge you in all things in life to lean into Him, let go, and let God move in His mighty ways. You will never be disappointed, and you truly will learn that His ways are higher than ours. That we need the mind and perspective of Christ in our daily lives. For those of you who have not given your life to Christ, I pray as you read my story you will go to John 3:16 and pray for salvation and surrender to Him. For until we let go of our life and give it all to Christ, we will never know what living truly is. His way is the better way!

My final word of hope to you and this hurting world is First Corinthians 13, the love chapter in the Bible. Love and kindness in serving each other is the greatest hope and anchor we can give to one another. Love is never self-serving, prideful, jealous, full of wrong ambitions, lies, boastful, hording materials, exploitation, abuse, or controlling behaviors. True love is serving others from a pure heart, loving unconditionally. Proverbs 18:21 states, *"Death and life are in the power of the tongue, and those who love it will eat its fruits. Out of the abundance of our hearts the mouth speaks."* My gift to you is to encourage you to allow God to do surgery on your heart. Let your life be full of His desires and passions. You will not be sorry for what He brings to you.

One of the special songs the Lord put across my path was, "Tell Your Heart to Beat Again," by Danny Gokey. As you listen to that song, listen to his words behind that song. It is beautiful and reveals the beauty the Lord wants to bring to our lives and hearts. My prayers are that my story brings hope, healing, and a better way to your life. I hope it shows you that no matter what you're going through, what He calls you to do for His Purpose and Glory, anything we face in life to run to your Father who created you. He has created you, given you gifts and purpose. How are you stewarding these gifts? If we don't use them, we lose them, and miss out on what God has for us. Please join me and many others in helping to make this world a better place, to heal our nation, and bring hope to many again. I wish you peace, hope, love, and joy in your life.

One of my favorite sayings is: Learn, Laugh, Love, & Grow. That is what life is all about in Christ. Love and peace to all of you. Always remember that against all odds, there is hope when you lean into the Lord, give it all to Him, and let Him do His perfect work. Heart surgery spiritually makes you whole and gives you a brand new, full, wonderful life. God's Perfect Will! Blessings my friends.

EVERYDAY LEADERS

Everyday Leaders Professional Coaching and Consulting i an International Growth Company offering programs and services to organizations who are invested in building better leaders and maximizing potentials in life and business:

We do this through in person or virtual training, workshops and programs designed in:

    Personal and Professional Growth
    Leadership Development
    Communication
    Teamwork

Inspirational Speaking and Keynotes delivered on:

    Building Self Confidence, Igniting Clarity, Empowering Courage, and Becoming a Catalyst for Change.

    Melahni's 501C3 - Making Everyday Leaders, Inc. operates and facilitates Shortridge High School, Indianapolis, IN -Life Skills

Programs to Empower Developing at Risk Young Women Leaders.

Other Published Works as a contributing author include:

Mentoring Moments, 14 Remarkable Women Share Breakthroughs to Success

Pandemic Blessings, Stories of Thanksgiving in an Unusual Time

Voices for Leadership, Vol 1, Your Pathway to Becoming a More Influential Leader

The Impact of Influence, Vol 3, Ladies Using Their Influence to Create a Life of Impact

The Impact of Influence Vol 5, Using Your Influence to Make a Life of Impact

The Impact of Influence Vol 7, Overcoming Adversity to Make an Influence

The Impact of Community Partnerships:

USAF, The Strategies, JPtheGeek, Aspire Johnson County, Indiana Chamber Executives Association, Leadership Carroll County and the Carroll County Chamber of Commerce Women's Leadership Series, Fulton County Chamber of Commerce, Pass the Torch for Women Foundation, SCALE for Women, LLP, Life Service Center of America, LLC, The WHY Institute, Bauer Family Services, Association of Women Business Owners, Network of Women in Business, Top Floor Women, and Perry Township Religious Youth Association.

Certifications include:

John Maxwell Leadership, Speaker, Coach, and Trainer.

WHY Institute, Certified Coach and Corporate Consultant

Awards:

Aspire Johnson County, Woman Leader of the Year 2024

Finalist for Aspire Johnson County Champion for Women, 2023 and 2024

Finalist for Aspire Johnson County Woman Leader of the Year 2023

Community Builder Award, Evergreen Leadership, 2020

At Everyday Leaders, we believe:

"It's not what you do in a day, it's what you do every day that makes the most impact."

If you are ready to grow your heart and invest in your personal growth, join us. We meet you where you are and help you grow to where you want to be.

www.everydayleaders.com

Everyday Moments: Lessons that Transform Lives

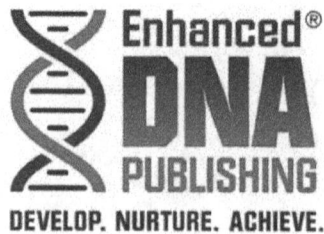

www.ingramcontent.com/pod-product-compliance
Lightning Source LLC
Chambersburg PA
CBHW050643160426
43194CB00010B/1787